Ultimate Price Guide to

FAST FOOD
COLLECTIBLES/

Edited by Elizabeth A. Stephan

© 1999 by
Krause Publications

Published by

**krause
publications**

700 E. State Street • Iola, WI 54990-0001
Telephone: 715/445-2214

Please, call or write us for our free catalog of antiques and collectibles publications. To place an
order or receive our free catalog, call 800-258-0929. For editorial comment and further information,
use our regular business telephone at (715) 445-2214

Library of Congress Catalog Number: 99-61255
ISBN: 0-87341-786-0

Printed in the United States of America

Contents

What's on the Cover

MIB

Arby's; Tasmanian Devil, Tweetie, Porky, Bugs Bunny, Yosemite Sam, Sylvester, Pepe Le Pew; Looney Tunes Figures (on base) $10

McDonald's; Toy Story with Woody figure; Walt Disney Home Video Masterpiece Collection 3

Hardee's; Smurf with orange board; Smurfin' Smurfs 9

McDonald's; Ronald Nite Stand Star Figure; Bedtime 6

McDonald's; Roller Blade; Barbie/Hot Wheels Mini-Streex 2

Hardee's; Alotta Stile in pink boots, Anita Break with package under her arm, Buster with skateboard, Benny bowling; California Raisins 7

Wendy's; Frosty; Fast Food Racers 4

Burger King; Balancer; Superman 5

Subway; Birthday Blue; Blue's Clues 4

McDonald's; Francis; A Bug's Life 2

McDonald's; 101 Dalmatians 10

Land Before Time; Burger King 6

Burger King; Maggie with turtle; Simpsons figures 8

Hardee's; Ren & Stimpy 3

Burger King; Mr. Potato Head 3

McDonald's; School Teacher; Recess 3

McDonald's; Pinchers the Lobster; Teenie Beanie Babies 4

Foreword

In 1996, Jeff and Marilyn Escue approached the Museum of Science and Industry to be the recipient of the largest and most comprehensive collection of fast food toys. It might seem that a museum founded on the lofty goals of science literacy would not be interested in such "pop culture." But after a short deliberation by our Collections Committee, it was decided that the materials fit closely with our goals, and that our visitors crave artifacts that are relevant to their everyday lives. Our new exhibit on fast food toys demonstrates how these little gems link popular culture, art and science.

Fast food toys not only provide amusement for children, and act as purchase incentives for hamburgers and fries on the go, they have become cultural icons that decorate desks, window sills and collector's shelves. As Jeff and Marilyn have shown me, these are not just little blobs of plastic but animated works of art that delight us with their creativity and whimsy. As a science museum, we wanted to illustrate to the public how these toys are made and operate. Our exhibit makes connections to manufacturing, from plastic or more likely Polyvinyl Chloride, and injection molds, to engineering and the tiny power sources that allow the toys to roll, walk or hop across the table. With one single collection we can document a broad range of American popular culture from cartoon characters to popular toys, movies and sports icons.

When I was small I admit to buying cereal for the toy inside, but my lick-on tattoo hardly compares to the colorful, creative and very artistic toys represented in our over 5,000-piece collection. One of the collection highlights is the Triple-Play Funmeal set, the first fast food toy which featured the then twenty-four major league baseball teams from the now-defunct Burger Chef restaurant from 1973. Few people

Mike Sarna is curator of the Museum of Science and Industry.

know that it was Burger Chef's promotions that caught the eye of McDonald's and change the way fast food was marketed to children and adults alike.

The collection not only includes toys but also boxes, bags and counter displays. In total, it encompasses fifteen boxes, and catalogers have been steadfastly working on the collection for over two years. Fast food toys are an emerging hobby that has mass appeal. With the inexpensive or free toy available from your neighborhood restaurant, people of all ages can join in the fun.

With any type of collecting comes a bit of nostalgia. You can look at the objects you have collected over the years and remember the challenge of obtaining them. This is certainly the case with fast food toys. Many people, including myself, have witnessed or participated in the lines waiting for a restaurant to open in order to secure that certain elusive treasure that rounds out the rest of a collection. You may have even been one of the many millions who searched for The Lion King set in 1994 or have participated in the Teenie Beanie Baby frenzies of recent years. In ten to twenty years you can look back at your collection and reminisce about those efforts, and you may even have one of the few rare toys that could increase substantially in value over time.

Collecting can begin at any age. That is especially true with fast food toys. They are inexpensive to purchase which allows children to participate in the fun of collecting. Adding to a fast food toy collection can also be a fun family activity. Families can go to toy conventions and shows to buy and trade toys, and also stop at the local neighborhood restaurant to pick up the latest set. Collectors can surf the Internet for toy information at over forty sites devoted to fast food toys. Most importantly, don't forget to buy extras of your favorite toys and use them as they were intended—play!

Michael T. Sarna, curator
Museum of Science and Industry
Chicago

Museum of Science and Industry, Chicago.

Introduction

Originally meant to attract kids and their parents to a restaurant, fast food toys have become the ideal collectible—easy to store, readily available, colorful, inexpensive and fun. In the last twenty-plus years, fast food restaurants have created a collecting goldmine. Most promotions run an average of four weeks with a new toy every week—that's fifty-two toys a year! And what is easier to collect than a little toy from a restaurant? Pull up to the drive-thru window, get dinner and a toy. It's almost like getting something for nothing—get a burger, get a beanbag. Pizza Hut will even deliver their promotions to your front door. (Of course you do have to buy a pizza.)

What is it about these tiny toys that we find so appealing? Why do we collect at all? Is it our inherent need to hunt and gather—the pursuit, the attack and the kill—that attracts us? Anyone who has participated in the madness caused by the introduction of the Teenie Beanie Baby promotions by McDonald's over the last three years would agree. Even true Beanie Baby haters stood in line and bought the least expensive item on the menu just to get their hands on whatever Teenie Beanie Baby was being offered that hour.

While McDonald's Teenie Beanie Babies may be the most popular fast food promotion in the short history of restaurant premiums and a perfect example of marketing, name recognition, and, yes, even greed, they are not the only sought-after premium out there. Who didn't want to make sure they had all of the California Raisins offered by Hardee's? Or all variations of the Smurfs offered by the same chain a few years later.

The average collector doesn't become so crazed as to believe they can find every single variation of every toy ever made, but they do want complete sets. Why do we do it? The memories. The socialization. The desire to capture a little of our own history.

Domino's Pizza uses their own characters such as The Noid in order to avoid licensing fees. Burger King and McDonald's have acquired licenses from Hanna-Barbera and Warner Brothers.

Fast Food as Social History

History? Yes, history.

Any armchair historian can see the reflection of our popular culture in the evolution of the fast food restaurants and their promotions. Fast food became popular during a time of change in American culture—the 1950s. Most fast food restaurants were drive-ins—the perfect place for the teen-age boy to show off his car and be cool. Kids were able to hang out, listen to rock 'n roll, plan drag races, and best of all, annoy their parents.

McDonald's emerged in the 1950s as a chain restaurant when the American family was beginning its exodus from the city. They were one of the first fast food establishments to set up in the newly-established suburbs, instantly making them popular with kids and parents alike. Other chains soon followed suit.

As society changed, fast food changed. American culture was drastically altered during the 1960s and '70s, and fast food chains began gearing their advertising budget away from the teen-age demographic to the under-ten crowd.

Restaurants have offered toys and promotions featuring their characters and mascots for years, but offering a premium and food as a packaged meal was still a new concept in the 1970s. Burger Chef started the trend in 1973 with the advent of the Funmeals. By using their own characters, Burger Chef was able to forego the legal headache and expensive fees associated with licensed products. This all changed in 1978.

Burger Chef offered two licensed Funmeals that year—the Triple-Play Funmeal and, more importantly, their *Star Wars* Funmeal. Catching the attention of the larger chains (i.e., McDonald's) with the Triple-Play Funmeal, Burger Chef scored

Boxes could easily be the sleeper of the fast food hobby.

big with the *Star Wars* promotion. It demonstrated how lucrative a licensed product could be.

McDonald's began test marketing the Happy Meal on a regional basis in 1977 and 1978. The Happy Meal made its national premiere with the *Star Trek* promotion in 1979. (Were they trying to cash in on the *Star Wars* craze with the other popular sci-fi license?) It was an instant success. Fast food would never be the same again.

It was during the 1980s that fast food premiums came into their own. Initially, restaurants used generic give-aways or their own characters as promotions. McDonald's had already established the McDonaldland characters, White Castle had the Castleburger Dudes. Sonic Drive-In developed toys based on their food items.

By the 1990s, licensing was the key to the success of a kid's meal promotion. Up to this point, McDonald's was the only restaurant with the clout to pull off a national campaign. Little by little, the other chains began to creep up on them, and it was Burger King's Lion King Kids Meal in 1994 that proved other restaurants could compete with McDonald's.

State of the Market

Toys aren't the only thing collectors want. Displays, boxes, bags and inserts are seen by many as the sleeper of the hobby. While the ephemera associated with fast food hasn't increased in value, it will. Paper disintegrates, especially when mixed with fries, hamburgers, condiments and children. Displays aren't readily available to the public and to get one, you need an "in" at the restaurant.

Toys are readily available at garage sales for pennies, but they aren't often in Mint condition. It is the search for the Mint toy that keeps the hobby healthy and active. A spotty collection can be filled in with flea-market finds, but a collector may have to search toy shows, scan the adds in *Toy Shop* magazine or search the Internet to find that Mint in Package toy. Collector clubs and conventions allows people to swap toys, exchange information and create friendships that can last a lifetime.

How to Use this Book

Most fast food toys are found individually, not in sets. It is for this reason that the **prices given are for the individual toys, not for the whole set.** The value for an entire set can be figured by adding the values of the individual toys. Under 3 (U3) toys are listed separate from the regular promotions because they often carry a different value.

The items listed in the book were compiled with the help of public relations offices of many fast food chains and months of research. Toy shows, ads in *Toy Shop*, and our fast food toy consultant, Jeff Escue, were the primary sources for the pricing you'll find in this book.

Thank You

This book wasn't done alone.

Many of the toys you see are part of the Museum of Science and Industry's collection and will become part of a permanent display in November 1999. *Toy Shop* editor Sharon Korbeck and I spent the day in Chicago working with photographer Joe Ziolkowski and his assistant Jamie Isberner as they set up and shot over 500 toys. Curator Mike Sarna, Archivist Laura H. Graedel and Curatorial Assistant Natalia Bednarek, all involved with the cataloging and gathering of this massive collection, made us feel at home and showed us how one the most well-known museums in the country works on the inside.

Krause Publications' expert photographers Ross Hubbard, Kris Kandler and Bob Best photographed toys supplied by area collectors and dealers. Tom Michael, Pam Stiles, Joey Hedrington, Sharon Korbeck, Maggie Thompson, Jon Brecka and Joel Edler donated many of the toys pictured on these pages. Hubbard also set up and photographed the cover; designed by Kevin Sauter, the cover surpasses all others. Bonnie Teztlaff, Cheryl Hayburn and Cheryl Mueller of book production did a fine job with the layout of the pages and scanning of the photos.

Jeff Escue, a long-time contributor to *Toys & Prices* and a collector of fast food toys, lent his expertise, opinion and knowledge of prices. A gentleman in every sense of the word, Jeff made this book possible. Paul Browning, collector of everything Burger Chef, compiled listings and photographs for the Burger Chef chapter.

Thanks also goes out the home offices of several fast food chains, their public relations and kid's meal promotions staff, including: Angela Strum from KFC, Chandra Streifel from Taco Bell, Lynn Apuzzo from Subway, Bruce Hinton, Jr. from Long John Silver's, Amy Murray from McDonald's, and Charles Nicolas and Kim Miller from Burger King. Those listed were able to provide comprehensive lists of toys and photographs, and they were able to answer my numerous questions regarding the world of fast food restaurants and premiums.

Be Careful Out There

Long-time collectors know that a price guide is just that—a guide. Also keep in mind that the dealers will pay less than book value for an item because they have to mark it up in order to make a profit. A price guide is best used as a tool to gauge the popularity and demand for an item.

Price guides can be helpful, but they can also be frustrating. Prices can vary widely from source to source, depending on geographical differences, personal economics and target market. Remember, prices listed in this book are not offers to buy or sell any of these items. Hopefully this book will assist you in the way it was intended—as a guide to gauge the value of your toys.

Elizabeth A. Stephan, editor
stephane@krause.com

The Greatest Fast Food Toys

In the more than twenty-year history of fast food toy premiums, hundreds of toys have been offered by more than thirty restaurants. Many of the toys have been played with, discarded and long forgotten. Others are enjoying a healthy life on the secondary market, as favorites for collectors.

Listed below are some of the most important fast food premiums of all time. Some of these sets are common and of little value but are included because they may have had a powerful impact on the fast food hobby as we know it today. Toys are listed alphabetically by restaurant.

Note: Scarceness comparisons to McDonald's are base on attending shows and examining secondary market sales. McDonald's tends to lead the pack in promotion of toys, and the company also has more stores, about 12,000 in the United States compared with 6,000 each for Burger King, Wendy's, Pizza Hut and KFC, 2,500 for Arby's and 500 for White Castle.

Arby's

Looney Tunes, figures on base, 1987, set of seven. This chain has done a few truly great-looking promos, and combined with the fact that they sell few premiums gives the collector scarcity. In 1987-1989, Arby's ran successive Looney Tunes promotions. Many of these sets are quite rare, although not at all expensive, yet. The most interesting of these sets is the 1987 set of seven figures on oval bases featuring Bugs Bunny, Porky Pig, Yosemite Sam, Sylvester, Tweety, Tasmanian Devil and Pepe Le Pew.

This is one of the the only sets to feature Pepe; this romantic skunk seems to have only been issued in a few regional markets while the other pieces were issued nationally.

If Pepe (with his limited distribution) were a McDonald's piece, it would sell for over $100 loose. Why is this set so important? As the collecting base becomes more knowledgeable, they will recognize this set's tremendous detail and quality and its relative scarcity combined with Pepe's outright rarity.

This set is about forty times scarcer than McDonald's nationally-issued sets from this same period. At least four different boxes were issued. They have tremendous graphics and sell for about $20 each.

Arby's Looney Tunes on base. The Pepe Le Pew alone is valued at $75.

Burger Chef

Funmeal boxes, 1973, set of twenty-four. Because it was the first kid's meal promotion, this set ranks number one on the list. In general, these boxes were often thrown out immediately. These boxes featured punch-out characters, games, great graphics in full color combined with Burger Chef's own characters—Burgerilla the gorilla, The Great Burgerini the magician, Blueburger the pirate, Fangburger the vampire, Crankenburger the monster, Jeff the Burger Chef worker and Chef the cook.

Triple Play Funmeal #1 open game board, 1977, twenty-four-box set. These included one box for each major league team, with nine punch-out baseball player discs. Each disc featured a player for the respective team.

This was the first licensed set, and it is very scarce today.

The key to this set's collectibility is that some discs featured future Hall of Fame players. These sell for substantially more than boxes without these discs.

All boxes were issued in identical quantities and were available at all stores simultaneously.

***Star Wars*, 1978, set of six boxes.** This really caught the eye of the public...and the competition. The *Star Wars* license was the key here; this was the first restaurant set to be tied to a major motion picture. It really opened the industry's eyes to the potential of movie licensing, confirming the earlier aforementioned success of the major league baseball license of the Triple-Play-Funmeal box set.

The *Star Wars* set had punch-out characters and games combined with great color graphics. These boxes are more common at *Star Wars* shows than at fast food shows.

Burger King

Lion King, 1994 set of seven. The release of this set was a defining moment in the modern fast food toy hobby because it ensured competition among the restaurant chains. This Disney licensed promo sold out in two or three weeks versus the expected seven-week promo period.

Burger King's Lion King promotion for 1994 was an eye-opener to McDonald's.

Burger King made many of these toys, reportedly over fifty million total for the first promo. (The promo was so successful it was reissued later in the year).

In one fell swoop, the hobby had a race going between Burger King and McDonald's. For most of the 1980s and early 1990s, this was not the case.

Burger King devastated the competition's sales during this toy promo. From this point forward, all restaurants took a different look at the kid's meal concept.

Toy Story, 1995, set of six. This set was a continuation of Burger King's awakening to licensing. This set was an awesome success, as was the movie. The army men are impossible to find loose; expect a premium in the future for them.

Hardee's

California Raisins, 1987, set of four. An enormously popular fad, the Raisins exemplified the power of hitting while the subject's hot. This promotion got people of all ages into the stores.

But Hardee's didn't always have perfect timing with fads. Its later "Where's Waldo" promotion flopped.

Smurfs, 1987, over 100 figures. This set was fascinating since over 100 Smurfs were issued. The little blue people helped take away the blues for young and old alike.

Jack In The Box

Jack, 1996, set of three. Jack the round-headed corporate guy was quite cool. It's the first set issued that made light of the chain's own corporate management. This regional set was only available west of the Mississippi River, where the chain has stores. This set is about forty times scarcer than McDonald's nationally-issued sets from this same period.

Kentucky Fried Chicken (KFC)

Garfield, 1996, set of six. KFC finally joined the hunt with a well-done set of toys based on Jim Davis's feline comic character. The figures sat in tiny wheeled vehicles. This set is about thirty times scarcer than McDonald's nationally-issued sets from this period

Lee's Fried Chicken

Cartoon Viewers, 1980s, set of six. This toy worked like a tiny View-Master viewer. Superman, Mighty Mouse, Bugs, Porky, Popeye and Woody Woodpecker cartoons were produced.

Lee's restaurants are located primarily east of the Mississippi, so this was a very limited regional promotion. Bugs and Porky are more common than the others. This set is about 100 times scarcer than McDonald's nationally-issued sets from this period.

McDonald's

Star Trek, 1979, set of fifteen. This was the awakening of a giant. After Burger Chef caught their attention with their early successes, McDonald's came up with this idea—a great idea with good execution for the time.

History may show, however, that McDonald's thought the success of Burger Chef's *Star Wars* promotion was because it was space related, rather than the fact that it was *Star Wars*.

McDonald's later tried other space themes that bombed and probably thought the whole thing, including their own success with the *Star Trek* promo, was a fluke.

This promo also represented the move to plastic in the form of rings, navigator bracelets and communicators. Also included was a paper board game only issued loose and iron-on patches.

Astrosniks, 1983, set of eight. This was a regional promotion, important because it was the first high quality licensed follow-up to the successful 1979 *Star Trek* promo.

Lots of toys were issued between 1979 and 1983 with nothing significant from a collector's point of view. In spite of *Star Trek*'s success, McDonald's didn't follow through with the concept of a great kid's meal promo. Neither did any one else.

New Archies, 1988, set of six. Besides being great looking, this set featured the ever-popular Archies comic book characters. Issued within about 300 miles of St. Louis, Mo., this is one of the best regional toys McDonald's ever produced.

Prior to 1992, most sets were issued nationally with a few regional sets. McDonald's decided to issue all toys nationally in 1992.

Black History, 1988, set of two coloring books. This was the first major attempt to offer a promo for a minority audience. Issued only at a few inner city Detroit restaurants, these items are very rare. These items have sold for up to three times book price ($500) at auction, which brought a few out of the woodwork.

Mac Tonight, 1988, set of six. Mega cool Mac Tonight was the first rock star of fast food. This moon-faced crooner was popularized in nationwide advertising.

United Airlines, 1991, set of two. This was the first kid's meal that actually flew airlines passengers—kind of a wild concept if you think about it. The toys are well done featuring Ronald and Grimace in identical white United Airlines airplanes; more recent ones were gray. Press down on the characters, and the planes went rolling.

United Airlines offered this promotion out of major airports. It carries a premium due to its scarcity.

101 Dalmatians, 1996, set of 101. This set was definitely created with the collector in mind, somewhat of a formal embracing of the hobby.

McDonald's sold the whole set in a custom box for about $120. This was a first. At least 50,000 boxed sets were sold.

Many collectors passed because they felt figures could be acquired or traded later. Big mistake. The boxed set now sells for over $300.

This toy was, for McDonald's relevance, issued with quantities normally attributed to a regional promotion, fewer than one million of each dog.

Teenie Beanie Babies, 1997, set of 10. Beanie Babies—the toy many love to hate. Yet this promotion sold about 100 million toys (ten million of each toy presumably) in less than two weeks instead of the five-week time slot allotted for the promo.

This was reported as the biggest-selling promotions in fast food history and has since inspired two more Teenie Beanie promotions.

Pizza Hut

Universal Monsters, 1991, set of three cups. These cups featured three-dimensional colored lids and a hologram card of the featured monster. The cups feature the Wolfman, Dracula and Frankenstein. The card was the first hologram issued with a fast food promo. As holograms continue to become more affordable, expect to see more used.

This set is about 100 times scarcer than McDonald's nationally-issued sets from this period.

Taco Bell

Star Wars, 1997, set of eight. This set contains one of the best toys ever issued—the Yoda/Darth Vader hologram cube. You have to see one to believe it. Tilt the cube one way you see a three-dimensional Yoda; tilt again and you see Darth Vader.

Darth Vader view of Taco Bell's Yoda/ Darth Vader hologram cube.

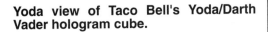

Yoda view of Taco Bell's Yoda/Darth Vader hologram cube.

Wendy's

Felix the Cat, 1996, set of six. Wendy's offered some high quality sets in the mid-1980s. What is important about this set is that after a five-year dry spell, Wendy's came back with a knockout set featuring the fabulous frenetic feline.

The bags the kid's meals were sold in are some of the best. Wendy's bag featured high quality graphics on coated stock glossy paper finish. The artwork was spectacular even on generic promotions.

White Castle

Castle Meal Friends, 1990, set of six. This regional hamburger chain pulls a rabbit out of a hat every now and then. Castle Meal Friends were White Castle's own characters. They were well made with very limited distribution.

This set proved that a small chain can do creative work related to their own characters' creation.

This set is about fifty times scarcer than McDonald's nationally-issued sets from this same period.

Fat Albert and the Cosby Kids, 1990, set of four. This is a classic featuring the licensed Cosby characters. Fat Albert was produced in smaller quantities than the other three characters. Hold him in your hand and you will see why. He weighs a ton, figuratively speaking. This has got to be the heaviest toy ever produced for a fast food restaurant.

This set is also important because it is one of the few sets featuring African-American characters.

This set is about fifty times scarcer than McDonald's nationally-issued sets from this same period. This set was reissued once. No boxes or bags were issued with this promo.

Arby's

Founded by brothers Forrest and Leroy Raffel, the first Arby's opened in Boardman, Ohio on July 23, 1964 with a menu limited to roast beef sandwiches, potato chips and beverages. The Raffels, founders of Raffel Brothers, Inc., a food service consulting firm, wanted to develop a fast food chain based on something other than hamburgers. After witnessing and taking part in a huddled mass waiting for 79-cent roast beef sandwiches, they knew they'd found their product. Several different names, including Big Tex, were tossed around before they settled on Arby's, which stands for Raffel Brothers, R.B. not "roast beef" as some have speculated. Arby's has since grown from only two stores in 1965 to over 3,000 worldwide.

Their involvement with kid's premiums dates back to 1981 when they issued the Little Miss and Mr. Men figures. In Mint condition, these figures can go for as much as $10 apiece.

Arby's has done several spectacular premiums. The two that have the highest collector value are the successive Looney Tunes sets from 1987-1989. Bugs Bunny, Daffy Duck, Taz, Elmer Fudd, Road Runner and Wile E. Coyote were the six free-standing figures that made up the initial set. The second set is considered by some collectors as one of the best fast food promotions ever done. This time around the Bugs and the gang were on oval bases, and included one seldom seen character, Pepe Le Pew. Pepe is rarely, if ever, included in Looney Tunes sets, and his inclusion here seems to have been done on a regional basis. Pepe alone is valued at $75 in Mint condition.

The Babar's World Tour promotion from 1990-1991 includes toys worth from $2-$5 in Mint condition, but the boxes are the real treasure. The series included as many as fifteen boxes, each documenting Babar's adventures as he traveled the globe. The colorful and interesting graphics are why these boxes can sell for up to $10 each.

TOY NAME	DESCRIBE	YEAR	EX	MINT
Babar's World Tour at the Beach Summer Sippers set of three squeeze bottles: orange, yellow or purple top		1991	1	5
Babar's World Tour Finger Puppets set of four: King Babar, Queen Celeste, Alexander & Zephyr, Pom		1990	3	5
Babar's World Tour License Plates set of four: Paris, Brazil, USA, North Pole		1990	1	2
Babar's World Tour Puzzles set of four: Cousin Arthur's New Camera, Babar's Gondola Ride, Babar, the Haunted Castle, Babar's Trip to Greece		1990	2	4
Babar's World Tour Racers set of three pull-back racers: King Babar, Cousin Arthur, Queen Celeste		1992	2	4

TOY NAME	DESCRIBE	YEAR	EX	MINT
Babar's World Tour Squirters set of three			1	3
Babar's World Tour Stampers set of three: Babar, Flora, Arthur		1990	2	4

Babar's World Tour Storybooks
    set of three: Read Get Ready, Set, Go,
    Calendar-Read and Have Fun-Read,
    Grow and Grow
		1991	1	2

Babar's World Tour Vehicles
    set of three vehicles: Babar in helicopter,
    Arthur on trike, Zephyr in car
		1990	2	4

Classic Fairy Tales
    set of three: Jack and the Beanstalk, The 3
    Little Pigs, Hansel and Gretel
		1993	2	4

Little Miss Figures
    set of eight: Little Miss Giggles, Little Miss
    Helpful, Little Miss Shy, Little Miss
    Splendid, Little Miss Late, Little Miss
    Naughty, Little Miss Star, Little Miss
    Sunshine
		1981	4	10

Little Miss Stencil		1985	15	25

Babar's World Tour Vehicles, Arby's, 1990. Photo courtesy Museum of Science and Industry, Chicago.

Little Miss Figures, Arby's, 1981. Photo courtesy Museum of Science and Industry, Chicago.

! Remember, prices given are for individual pieces only, not complete sets.

Little Miss Stencil, Arby's, 1985. Photo courtesy Museum of Science and Industry, Chicago.

Looney Tunes Car-Tunes, Arby's, 1989.

Looney Tunes Figures, Arby's, 1988. Photo courtesy Museum of Science and Industry, Chicago.

TOY NAME	DESCRIBE	YEAR	EX	MINT
Looney Tunes Figure (on base) Pepe Le Pew (part of 1987 set)		1987	25	75
Looney Tunes Car-Tunes set of six: Sylvester's Cat-illac, Daffy's Dragster, Yosemite Sam's Rackin Frackin Wagon, Taz's Slush Musher, Bugs Buggy, Road Runner's Racer		1989	3	6
Looney Tunes Figures set of six free-standing figures: Bugs Bunny, Daffy Duck, Taz, Elmer Fudd, Road Runner, Wile E. Coyote		1988	3	6
Looney Tunes Figures (on base) set of seven figures on oval base: Tasmanian Devil, Tweetie, Porky, Bugs Bunny, Yosemite Sam, Sylvester		1987	4	10
Looney Tunes Flicker Rings set of four rings: Bugs Bunny, Yosemite Sam, Porky Pig, Daffy Duck		1987	20	40
Looney Tunes Fun Figures set of three: Tazmanian Devil as pilot, Daffy as student, Sylvester as fireman		1989	3	6

Looney Tunes Flicker Rings, Arby's, 1987. Photo courtesy Museum of Science and Industry, Chicago.

Looney Tunes Fun Figures, Arby's, 1989. Photo courtesy Museum of Science and Industry, Chicago.

! Remember, prices given are for individual pieces only, not complete sets.

Looney Tunes Holiday Figures, Arby's, 1989. Photo courtesy Museum of Science and Industry, Chicago.

Looney Tunes Pencil Toppers, Arby's, 1988. Photo courtesy Museum of Science and Industry, Chicago.

Mr. Men Figures, Arby's, 1981. Photo courtesy Museum of Science and Industry, Chicago.

Yogi & Friends Winter Wonderland Crazy Cruisers, Arby's, 1995. Photo courtesy Museum of Science and Industry, Chicago.

TOY NAME	DESCRIBE	YEAR	EX	MINT
Looney Tunes Holiday Figures 　　set of three: Bugs as Santa, Porky Pig as 　　toy soldier, Tweety as elf		1989	4	8
Looney Tunes Pencil Toppers 　　set of six: Sylvester, Yosemite, Porky Pig, 　　Bugs Bunny, Taz, Daffy Duck, Tweety Bird		1988	5	10
Megaphone, Minnesota Twins 25th Anniversary		1986	1	2
Mr. Men Figures 　　set of ten: Mr. Bounce, Mr. Bump, Mr. 　　Daydream, Mr. Funny, Mr. Greedy, Mr. 　　Mischeif, Mr. Nosey, Mr. Rush, Mr. Strong, 　　Mr. Tickle		1981	3	10
Polar Swirl Penguins 　　set of four: penguin with mask and snorkle, 　　penguin with headphones, penguin with 　　sunglasses, penguin with surfboard		1987	15	40
Yogi & Friends Fun Squirters 　　set of three: Yogi, Cindy, Boo-Boo		1994	2	4
Yogi & Friends Mini-Disk 　　set of four: Ranger Smith, Yogi, Cindy, 　　Snagglepus		1993	1	2
Yogi & Friends Winter Wonderland Crazy Cruisers 　　Yogi, Snagglepuss, Cindy		1995	2	4

Boxes

Babar's World Tour Adventure Meal 　　Box 1: Train—Atlanta to New York		1990	5	10
Babar's World Tour Adventure Meal 　　Box 3: Submarine—London to Paris		1990	5	10
Babar's World Tour Adventure Meal 　　Box 4: Car—Paris to London		1990	5	10
Babar's World Tour Adventure Meal 　　Box 5: Boat—Venice to Egypt		1990	5	10
Babar's World Tour Adventure Meal 　　Box 6: Camel—Egypt to Russia		1990	5	10
Babar's World Tour Adventure Meal 　　Box 7: Truck—Russia to Japan		1990	5	10
Babar's World Tour Adventure Meal 　　Box 8: Sailboat—Japan to Australia		1990	5	10
Babar's World Tour Adventure Meal 　　Box 10: Whale—South Pole to China		1991	5	10

! Remember, prices given are for individual pieces only, not complete sets.

Babar's World Tour Adventure Meal Box 1 (front), Arby's, 1990.

Babar's World Tour Adventure Meal Box 1 (back), Arby's, 1990.

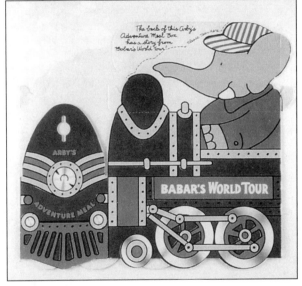

Babar's World Tour Adventure Meal Box 3, Arby's, 1990.

TOY NAME	DESCRIBE	YEAR	EX	MINT
Babar's World Tour Adventure Meal Box 11: Tour Bus: China to India		1991	5	10
Babar's World Tour Adventure Meal Box 12: India to Kenya		1991	5	10
Babar's World Tour Adventure Meal Box 13: Prop Plane: Kenya to Casablanca		1991	5	10
Babar's World Tour Adventure Meal Box 14: Yacht—Casablanca to Brazil		1991	5	10

Looney Tunes Adventure Meal
        Featuring Looney Tunes Friends in 'Good
        Knight Bugs Bunny'
		1987	20	30

Babar's World Tour Adventure Meal Box 4 (front), Arby's, 1990.

Babar's World Tour Adventure Meal Box 4 (back), Arby's, 1990.

! Remember, prices given are for individual pieces only, not complete sets.

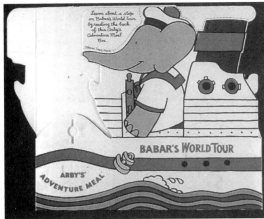

Babar's World Tour Adventure Meal Box 5 (front), Arby's, 1990.

Babar's World Tour Adventure Meal Box 5 (back), Arby's, 1990.

Babar's World Tour Adventure Meal Box 6 (front), Arby's, 1990.

Babar's World Tour Adventure Meal Box 6 (back), Arby's, 1990.

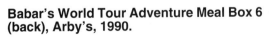

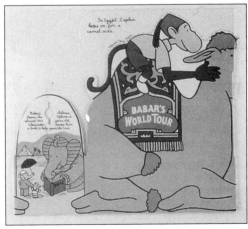

Babar's World Tour Adventure Meal Box
7 (front), Arby's, 1990.

Babar's World Tour Adventure Meal Box
7 (back), Arby's, 1990.

Babar's World Tour Adventure Meal Box 8
(front), Arby's, 1990.

Babar's World Tour Adventure Meal Box 8
(back), Arby's, 1990.

! Remember, prices given are for individual pieces only, not complete sets.

Babar's World Tour Adventure Meal Box 10 front), Arby's, 1991.

Babar's World Tour Adventure Meal Box 10 (back), Arby's, 1990.

Babar's World Tour Adventure Meal Box 11 (front), Arby's, 1991.

Babar's World Tour Adventure Meal Box 11(back), Arby's, 1991.

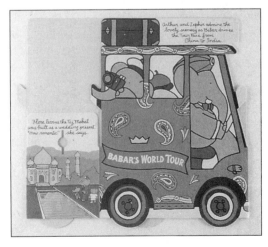

Babar's World Tour Adventure Meal Box 12 (front), Arby's, 1991.

Babar's World Tour Adventure Meal Box 12 (back), Arby's, 1990.

Babar's World Tour Adventure Meal Box 13 (front), Arby's, 1991.

Babar's World Tour Adventure Meal Box 13 (back), Arby's, 1991.

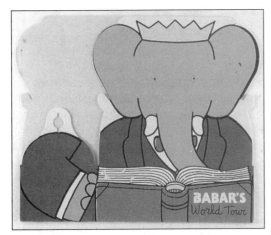

Babar's World Tour Adventure Meal (front), Arby's, 1991.

Babar's World Tour Adventure Meal (back), Arby's, 1991.

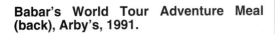

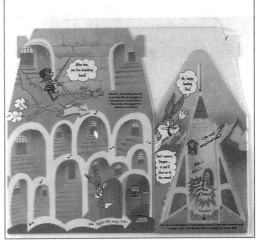

Looney Tunes Adventure Meal (back), Arby's.

Looney Tunes Adventure Meal (back), Arby's.

Burger Chef

Started in Indianapolis, Indiana, in 1954, the first Burger Chef was used as an equipment showcase for the restaurant equipment firm of General Equipment Manufacturing Company. By 1958, there were eight stores in Indiana, Illinois and Wisconsin. When Hardee's purchased the food chain in 1982, Burger Chef was a successful fast food chain with 650 restaurants in thirty-six states.

Thought of by many collectors as the founder of the kid's meal, Burger Chef forever changed the attitude of other restaurants towards marketing, product licensing, and their consumer base when the Funmeal was introduced in 1973.

Using their own characters—Burgerilla the gorilla, The Great Burgini the magician, Blueburger the pirate, Fangburger the vampire, Crankenburger the monster, Jeff the Burger Chef worker and Chef the cook—Burger Chef was able to bypass any licensing fees. These early Funmeals, featuring punch-out characters, games, colorful graphics, were usually thrown out and have became one of the most collectible items of all fast food premiums.

In 1977, they did their first licensed set—the Triple-Play Funmeal. The series of twenty-four boxes, each featuring nine punch-out baseball player discs, opened the eyes on many in the industry to the world of product licensing.

Burger Chef changed fast food promotions forever when they teamed up with Lucasfilm to offer a set of six *Star Wars* Funmeal boxes in 1978. Also offered was a set of two *Star Wars* poster in 1978 and three *Empire Strikes Back* posters in 1980. This was the first fast food tie-in with a major motion picture, and it caught the eye of everyone—including McDonald's, who had reportedly been toying with their own kid's meal after the success of Burger Chef's Triple-Play Funmeal.

Burger Chef's contribution to the world of fast food premiums can be felt today as restaurants vie for lucrative licensing contracts with movie studios and toy companies like Lucasfilm, Disney, Warner Brothers, Mattel and Hasbro. McDonald's, Burger King, Taco Bell, to name a few, use these little toys to draw in the young and old alike.

Contributor: Paul Browning, pbrowning@clarksville.com, www.burgerchef.com.

TOY NAME	DESCRIBE	YEAR	EX	MINT
Build a Burger Iron-ons	set of six: Bashful Buns, Chompin' Cheese Patty, Crying Onions, Mighty Mustard, Puckering Pickles, Tempting Tomatoes; allowed you to build your own sandwhich with iron-ons	1970s	5	10
Burger Chef & Jeff Glass	single glass; not part of a collection features Burger Chef and Jeff standing	1975	5	10
Burgerilla Hand Puppet	features Burgerilla character	1970s	5	10

! Remember, prices given are for individual pieces only, not complete sets.

Burgerilla Window Clinger, Burger Chef, 1970s. Photo courtesy Paul Browning.

Coin, Burger Chef, 1960s. Photo courtesy Paul Browning.

Burger Chef & Jeff Glass, Burger Chef, 1975. Photo courtesy Paul Browning.

Coins, Funmoney, Burger Chef, 1970s. Photo courtesy Paul Browning.

Crankenburger Iron-on, Burger Chef, 1978. Photo courtesy Paul Browning.

TOY NAME	DESCRIBE	YEAR	EX	MINT
Burgerilla Iron-on small iron-on of the Burgerilla Character		1978	5	10
Burgerilla Window Clinger features Burgerilla; 2" x 3"		1970s	5	10
Burgerini Hand Puppet features Burgerini character		1970s	5	10
Coin set of two wooden nickels: came in two different styles; used for five cents off any purchase made in a Burger Chef		1960s	2	4
Coins, Funmoney silver coins with pictures of several characters: Burger Chef & Jeff, Fangburger, Burgerilla; used for five cents off any purchase made in a Burger Chef		1970s	3	6
Crankenburger Iron-on small iron-on of the Crankenburger Character		1978	5	10

Crankenburger Window Clinger, Burger Chef, 1970s. Photo courtesy Paul Browning.

Family Circus Pinbacks, Burger Chef. Photo courtesy Paul Browning.

! Remember, prices given are for individual pieces only, not complete sets.

Friendly Monsters Glasses, Burger Chef, 1977. Photo courtesy Paul Browning.

Insert found inside large Flying Disk. Photo courtesy Paul Browning.

Flying Disk, small, Burger Chef, 1970s. Photo courtesy Paul Browning.

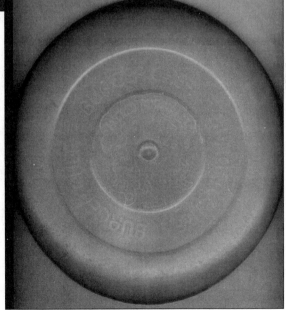

Flying Disk, large, Burger Chef, 1970s. Photo courtesy Paul Browning.

TOY NAME	DESCRIBE	YEAR	EX	MINT
Crankenburger Window Clinger features Crankenburger; 2" x 3"		1970s	5	10
Family Circus Comic Book "Adventures of The Family Circus"; may have been part of the Pinback collection			5	10
Family Circus Pinbacks set of six different pinbacks: featured character from The Family Circus: Daddy, Jeffy, Dolly, Billy, PJ and Mommy			5	10
Family Classics Cards There were reportedly over 90 cards in the series; each card had scenes from the following animated series: Arabian Nights, Swiss Family Robinson, Tom Sawyer, Snow White, Cinderella, Hiawatha, Puss in Boots, Johnny Appleseed, Paul Bunyon		1970s	5	10
Flying Disk, large non-glow in the dark; came in various colors; some picture Burger Chef & Jeff, some are only marked "Burger Chef"; 10" dia.		1970s	4	8
Flying Disk, large flying Saucer, glow in the dark; pictures Burger Chef & Jeff and marked "Incrediburgible!"; approx. 10" dia.		1972	4	8

Go Fish Card Game, Burger Chef, 1978-on. Photo courtesy Paul Browning.

! Remember, prices given are for individual pieces only, not complete sets.

Hand Puppet, Burger Chef, 1960s. Photo courtesy Paul Browning.

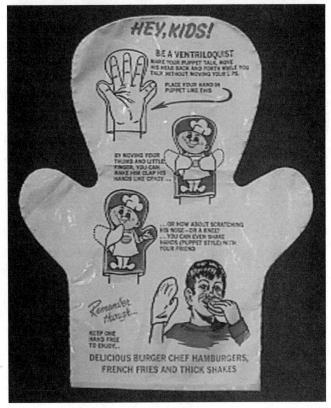

TOY NAME	DESCRIBE	YEAR	EX	MINT
Flying Disk, small	drink Lid: smaller non-glow in the dark version featuring Bugrer Chef characters and marked "Incrediburgible"; various colors	1970s	4	8
Friendly Monsters Glasses	set of six: Burger Chef & Jeff Go Trail Riding, Burgerilla Falls in Love, Burgerini's Rabbit Hops Away, Crankenburger Scores a Touchdown, Fangburger Gets a Scare, Werewolf Goes Skateboarding	1977	5	10

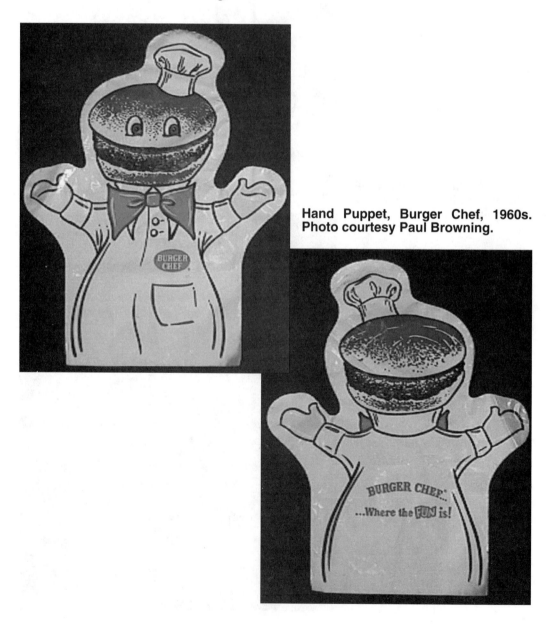

Hand Puppet, Burger Chef, 1960s. Photo courtesy Paul Browning.

NFL Collectors Series Glasses, Burger Chef, 1979. Photo courtesy Paul Browning.

President & Patriots Series Glasses, Burger Chef, 1975. Photo courtesy Paul Browning.

TOY NAME	DESCRIBE	YEAR	EX	MINT
Fun 'n Games Booklet			15	25
	Star Wars			
Fun Village Funmeal Boxes		1973-74	25	60
	set of 24 featuring Burger Chef characters			
Funburger Box		1972	50	75
	precursor to the Funmeal; came with puzzles on the box, and a prize inside; various			
Funburger Prize No. 30		1974	8	15
	Crankenburger Bike Flag, features Burger Chef logo on reverse			
Funburger Prize No. 4		1972	8	15
	car type 1: small blue car with marble in bottom to help roll			
Funburger Prize No. 4		1972	8	15
	car type 2: small blue car with marble in bottom to help roll.			

Playing Cards, Burger Chef. Photo courtesy Paul Browning.

! Remember, prices given are for individual pieces only, not complete sets.

Riddler, Burger Chef.
Photo courtesy Paul
Browning.

Star Spangled Funmeal
Trays, Burger Chef,
1976. Photo courtesy
Paul Browning.

TOY NAME	DESCRIBE	YEAR	EX	MINT
Funmeal Prize Deep Sea Treasure Search		1981	5	10
Funmeal Prize Puzzle set of at least three: different puzzles featuring Burger Chef & Jeff in different situations with different characters; puzzles were 4 piece x 4 piece		1972	5	15
Go Fish Card Game regular sized cards		1978-on	5	10
Halloween Bag given to children for Halloween; no copyright on bag		1978	5	10
Hand Puppet features character with a hamburger for a head; character unknown		1960s	10	15
Hand Puppet features 1960s Burger Chef character used in the logo		1960s	10	15
Klickety Klips small bag of colored straw bits to be put on bicycle spokes; came with small sticker sheet		1971	5	10
NFL Collectors Series Glasses set of 24 different NFL football team glasses: each smoky-colored glass has a football helmet with team logo		1979	5	10

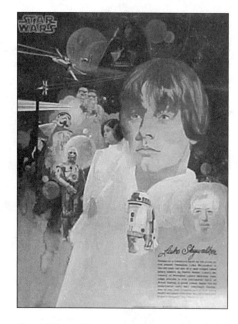 

Star Wars Posters, Burger Chef, 1977. Photo courtesy Paul Browning.

! Remember, prices given are for individual pieces only, not complete sets.

Super Shef Kite, Burger Chef. Photo courtesy Paul Browning.

TOY NAME	DESCRIBE	YEAR	EX	MINT
Old Maid Card Game features pictures of items and characters from Burger Chef; deck measured 1" x 1/2"		1978-on	5	10
Playing Cards featured picture of a pre-1970s Burger Chef on reverse side; nighttime photo; standard for playing cards size			5	10
President & Patriots Series Glasses set of six glasses featuring presidents and patriots: George Washington, Abraham Lincoln, Paul Revere, Ben Franklin, John F. Kennedy, Thomas Jefferson; back of glass features Burger Chef & Jeff talking about each featured president/patriot		1975	5	10
Race Cars set of five vacuform car containers		1981	20	30
Record Monster Fun Records set of six records featuring various characters: "Transylvania's Big Game," "Wolfeburger's Problem," "Cackleburger Casts a Spell" "The Ghost of Grizzly Mountain," "Fangburger's Haunted Hotel," "Crankenburger, the Super Salesman"		1970s	5	10
Riddler toy has several riddles with answers on a wheel you turn; probably a funmeal toy			5	10
Star Spangled Funmeal Trays set of twelve: Spirit of St. Louis, Mayflower, Lincoln's Log Cabin, Independence Hall, Conestoga Wagon, Statue of Liberty, Model T, Saturn Rocket, Bald Eagle, The Riverboat, The Alamo, Tom Thumb Train; all were punchouts		1976	20	30
Star Wars Funmeal Boxes set of seven: Darth Vader's Card Game, Tie Fighter, X-Wing Fighter, Land Speeder, R2D2 Droid Puppet, C3PO Droid Puppet, Flight Game		1978	25	40
Star Wars Posters set of four posters featuring characters from Star Wars: Chewbacca, Droids, Luke Skywalker, and Darth Vader		1977	10	15

! Remember, prices given are for individual pieces only, not complete sets.

Yo-yo, Burger Chef, 1972. Photo courtesy Paul Browning.

TOY NAME	DESCRIBE	YEAR	EX	MINT
Star Wars Posters	set of three different posters: characters from The Empire Strikes Back	1980	5	10
Stickers Krazy Kreature	set of six stickers of various characters: Pickle-Potamus, Must-Ketcher, Tomater-Gator, Chimpan-Cheese, Mynah-Burg-Er, Apple Turtle-Over	1971	5	10
Super Shef Kite	diamond-shaped kite advertising the Super Shef sandwich		5	10
T-Strip Racers	set of two (A & B): each car featured a large rear wheel that turned when you pulled a T-strip thru it; various colors	1970s	5	10
Triple Play Funmeal Boxes	Cardinals, Mets, Orioles, Pirates, Red Sox, Reds, Royals, Yankees; rare	1972	15	20
Triple Play Funmeal Boxes	Angels; very rare	1972	50	80
Triple Play Funmeal Boxes	set of 24 featuring Major League Baseball teams: Astros, A's, Braves, Brewers, Cubs, Dodgers, Expos, Giants, Indians, Padres, Phillies, Rangers, Tigers, Twins, White Sox; each came with one of six different posters featuring the Burger Chef characters	1978	10	15
Village Funmeal Boxes	set of 24 village buildings: Antique Shop, Bakery Shop, Barn, Beauty Shop, Bike Shop, Burger Chef, Cape Cod, Castle, Cottage (2), Colonial, Gas Station, Grocery Shop, Hardware Store, Haunted House, Pirate Ship, Ranch (2), Toy Shop, Two Story (2), Shoe Shop	1975	20	30
Yo-yo	set of at least three yo-yos featuring Burger Chef & Jeff: white and red, white and yellow, blue and white	1972	10	20

❗ Remember, prices given are for individual pieces only, not complete sets.

Burger King

The original Burger King, located at 3090 NW 36th Street in Miami, Florida, was started by James McLamore and David Edgerton in 1954. By 1967 there were 274 restaurants in existence, 2,000 in 1977, and, in 1998, the 10,000th Burger King was opened in Sydney, Australia.

Burger King introduced their first kid's meal promotion in 1981. When they launched their Kids Club 1990, one million kids joined in the first two months.

Many of the early Kids Club toys featured the Kids Club characters—Boomer, I/Q, Jaws, Kid Vid and Snaps, and it was the *Toy Story* promotion that awakened Burger King to the wonders of product licensing. In the last few years, Burger King has established several lucrative licensees—Hasbro's Mr. Potato Head, Disney and the itsy bitsy Entertainment Company's Teletubbies.

Although McDonald's is considered the industry leader, Burger King has proven to be a competent competitor. Their 1994 *Lion King* promotion is considered by many to be one of the top fast food toys of all times because it proved they could go head-to-head with McDonald's. When *Toy Story* was released in 1995, Burger King jumped at the chance to issue toys that both kids and collectors would love.

Burger King will no doubt continue to produce and distribute some of the most attractive and desirable premiums available.

TOY NAME	DESCRIBE	YEAR	EX	MINT
Adventure Kits	set of four activity kits with crayons; Passport, African Adventure, European Escapades, Worldwide Treasure Hunt	1991	1	3
Aladdin	set of five figures: Jafar and Iago, Genie in lamp, Jasmine and Rajah, Abu, Aladdin and the Magic Carpet	1992	1	3
Aladdin Hidden Treasures	set of four: Jasmine, Aladdin, Abu, Iago	1994	2	5
Alf	set of four: joke and riddle disk, door knob card, sand mold, refrigerator magnet	1987	1	2
Alf Puppets	set of four puppets with records: Sporting with Alf, Cooking with Alf, Born to Rock, Surfing with Alf	1987	3	8
Alvin and the Chipmunks	set of three: super ball, stickers, pencil topper	1987	1	2

TOY NAME	DESCRIBE	YEAR	EX	MINT
Anastasia		1997	2	5
	set of six: Bouncing Bartok, Fiendish Flyer, Fall-Apart Rasputin, Beanie Bat Bartok, Collision Course Dimitri, Anya & Pooka			
Archie Cars		1991	1	3
	set of four: Archie in red car, Betty in aqua car, Jughead in green car, Veronica in purple car			
Barnyard Commandos		1991	1	2
	set of four: Major Legger Mutton in boat, Sgt. Shoat & Sweet in plane, Sgt. Wooley Pullover in sub, Pvt. Side O'Bacon in truck			
Beauty & the Beast		1991	2	5
	set of four PVC figures: Belle, Beast, Chip, Cogsworth			

Aladdin Insert, Burger King, 1992.

Alf Puppets, Burger King, 1987. Photo courtesy Museum of Science and Industry, Chicago.

! Remember, prices given are for individual pieces only, not complete sets.

Archie Cars, Burger King, 1991. Photo courtesy Museum of Science and Industry, Chicago.

Barnyard Commandos, Burger King, 1991.

Beauty & the Beast, Burger King, 1991. Photo courtesy Museum of Science and Industry, Chicago.

TOY NAME	DESCRIBE	YEAR	EX	MINT
Beetlejuice	set of six figures: Uneasy Chair, Head Over Heels, Ghost to Ghost TV, Charmer, Ghost Post, Peek A Boo Doo	1990	1	2
Bicycle Safety Fun Booklet			1	2
BK Kids Club Action Figures	set of four: Boomer, I/Q, Jaws, Kid Vid	1991	1	3
BK Kids Club All-Stars	set of five: All-Stars Boomer, All-Stars I/Q, All-Stars Jaws, All-Stars Kid Vid, All-Stars Snaps	1994	1	3
BK Kids Club Bug Riders	set of five: I/Q Caterpillar, Snaps Cricket, Lingo Spider, Boomer Fire Eye, Kid Vid Scorpian	1998	1	3

Beetlejuice, Burger King, 1990.

Beauty & the Beast, Burger King, 1991. Photo courtesy Museum of Science and Industry, Chicago.

! Remember, prices given are for individual pieces only, not complete sets.

BK Kids Club Bug Riders, Burger King, 1998.

BK Kids Club Pranks, Burger King, 1994.

BK Kids Club Transporters Insert, Boomer, Burger King, 1990.

TOY NAME	DESCRIBE	YEAR	EX	MINT
BK Kids Club Coolers set of five: Kid Vid, blue; Jaws, turquoise; Snaps, yellow; I/Q, red; Boomer, purple		1995	2	4
BK Kids Club Glo-Force set of five glow-in-the-dark figures with costumes: Jaws as scubdiver, Snaps with safari gear, I/Q as surgeon, Kid Vid as astronaut, Boomer with ski gear		1996	1	2
BK Kids Club Mini Sports Games set of four games: two catcher mitts with ball, football, basketball hoop with ball, inflatable soccer ball		1993	1	2

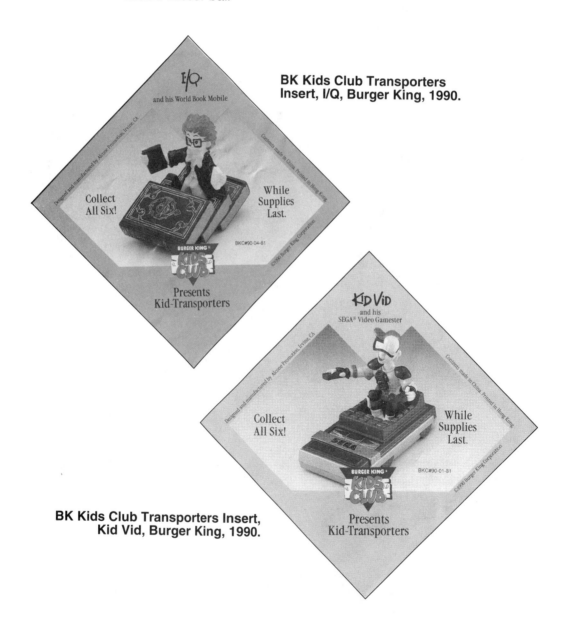

BK Kids Club Transporters Insert, I/Q, Burger King, 1990.

BK Kids Club Transporters Insert, Kid Vid, Burger King, 1990.

! Remember, prices given are for individual pieces only, not complete sets.

BK Kids Club Transporters Insert, Snaps, Burger King, 1990.

Capitol Critters, Burger King, 1992.

Captain Planet Flip-over Car, Burger King, 1991.

Captain Planet Flip-over Car: Hoggish Greedy, Burger King, 1991.

TOY NAME	DESCRIBE	YEAR	EX	MINT
BK Kids Club Planet Patrol Space Commander Jaws, I/Q's Planet Pacer, Boomer's Lightspeed Spacetop, Kid Vid's Glo Chopper, J.D. Shuttle Launch		1997	1	2
BK Kids Club Pranks set of five: Boomer's Joy Buzzer, Jaw's Spider, Kid Vid's Squirting Remote Control, Longo's Gumballs, I/Q's Whoopee Cushion		1994	1	3
BK Kids Club Transporters set of six: Snaps and her Camera Car, Boomer and her Super Shoe, I/Q and his World Book Mobile, Kid Vid and his SEGA Video Gamester		1990	2	4
BK Kids Club World Travel Adventure Kits set of four: Kid Vid's Mystery Treasure Map, Lingo's South American Quest, Jaw's African Adventure, Snap's Eupropean Escapade		1991	3	5

Chicago Bulls, Burger King, 1994. Photo courtesy Museum of Science and Industry, Chicago.

Disney Collector Series Tumblers, Burger King, 1994. Photo courtesy Burger King.

! Remember, prices given are for individual pieces only, not complete sets.

Disney Parade Figures, Burger King, 1991. Photo courtesy Museum of Science and Industry, Chicago.

Gargoyles II, Burger King, 1995. Photo courtesy Burger King.

Go-Go Gadget Gizmos Insert, Burger King, 1992.

TOY NAME	DESCRIBE	YEAR	EX	MINT
Bone Age Skeleton Kit set of four dinos: T-Rex, Dimetron, Mastadon, Similodon		1989	3	6
Bonkers Crash-Apart Cars set of five: Toots, Jitters, Fall-apart Rabbit, Piquel, Bonkers		1993	1	2
Burger King Clubhouse full size for kids to play in			15	35
Burger King Socks rhinestone accents			2	5
Calendar "20 Magical Years" Walt Disney World		1992	2	4
Capitol Critters set of four: Hemmet for Prez in White House, Max at Jefferson Memorial, Muggle at Lincoln Memorial, Presidential Cat		1992	1	2

Goof Troop Bowlers, Burger King, 1992.

Goofy Movie, Burger King, 1995.

 Remember, prices given are for individual pieces only, not complete sets.

Hunchback of Notre Dame Puppets, Burger King, 1996. Photo courtesy Burger King.

Land Before Time, Burger King, 1997.

Lion King Collectible Kingdom, Burger King, 1994. Photo courtesy Museum of Science and Industry, Chicago.

TOY NAME	DESCRIBE	YEAR	EX	MINT
Capitol Critters Cartons		1992	2	4
	punch-out masks: dog, chicken, duck, panda, rabbit, tiger, turtle			
Captain Planet		1991	1	2
	set of four flip-over vehicles: Captain Planet & Hoggish Greedily, Linka, Ma-Ti & Dr. Blight ecomobile, Verminous Skumm & Kwane helicopter, Wheeler and Duke Nukem snowmobile			
Captain Power		1988	8	10
	set of four plastic vacuform boxes: Powerjet Xt-7, Bio-Dread Patroller, Power Base, Phantom Striker			
Cartoon King Doll		1972	20	30
	16" tall; cloth			
Cartoon Network Racing Team		1997	1	2
	set of five: Speeding Bomber, Jeff Gordon Car, Scooby Doo Car, Burger King Race Car, Stoneage Rocker			

Lion King's Timon & Pumbaa, Burger King, 1996. Photo courtesy Burger King.

Little Mermaid Splash Collection, Burger King, 1993. Photo courtesy Museum of Science and Industry, Chicago.

! Remember, prices given are for individual pieces only, not complete sets.

M & M's Minis, Burger King, 1997.

Men in Black, Burger King, 1998.

Mickey's Toontown, Burger King, 1993.

TOY NAME	DESCRIBE	YEAR	EX	MINT
CatDog		1999	1	3
	set of five: Souped-up Skateboard, Crazy Catch Up, Gourmet Garbage Chaser, Key Catchin' Clock, Wacy Walker Upper			
Chicago Bull		1994	3	6
	set of four bendies: Stacey King #21, John Paxson #5, Scotti Pippen #33, BJ Armstrong #10; regionally distributed in Chicago area			
Chipmunk Adventure		1987	4	6
	set of four: bicycle licence plate, Alvin pencil topper, Alvin rubber ball, Sick 'Ems			
Christmas Crayola Bear		1986	5	8
	set of four bears: blue, red, yellow, red			
Christmas Crayola Bear Plush Toys		1986	3	6
	set of four: red, yellow, blue or purple			

Mr. Potato Head, Burger King, 1998.

Nerfuls, Burger King, 1989. Photo courtesy Museum of Science and Industry, Chicago.

! Remember, prices given are for individual pieces only, not complete sets.

Oliver & Company, Burger King, 1996. Photo courtesy Burger King.

Pocahontas Tumblers, Burger King, 1995. Photo courtesy Burger King.

Record Breakers Insert, Accelerator, Burger King, 1990.

TOY NAME	DESCRIBE	YEAR	EX	MINT
Christmas Sing-A-Long Cassette Tapes set of three Christmas sing-a-long tapes: Joy to the World/Silent Night, We Three Kings/O Holy Night, Deck the Halls/Night Before Christmas		1989	2	4
Crayola Coloring Books set of six books: Boomer's Color Chase, I/Q's Computer Code, Kids Club Poster, Jaws' Colorful Clue, Snaps' Photo Power, Kid Vid's Video Vision		1990	2	4
Crayola World Travel Adventure Kits set of four: Kid Vid's Tresure Map, Lingo's South American Quest, Jaw's African Adventure, Snap's European Escape		1991	2	5

Record Breakers Insert, Dominator, Burger King, 1990.

Record Breakers Insert, Fastlane, Burger King, 1990.

! Remember, prices given are for individual pieces only, not complete sets.

Record Breakers Insert, Indy, Burger King, 1990.

Record Breakers Insert, Shockwave, Burger King, 1990.

Record Breakers, Burger King, 1990.

TOY NAME	DESCRIBE	YEAR	EX	MINT
Dino Crawlers	set of five: blue, red, yellow, green, purple	1994	1	2
Dino Meals	punch-out sheets: Stegosaurus, Woolly Mammoth, T-Rex, Triceratops	1987	3	6
Disney 20th Anniversary Figures	set of four wind-up vehicles with connecting track: Minnie, Donald, Roger Rabbit, Mickey	1992	3	6
Disney Afternoon	set of four: Shovel, Treasure Chest, Sunshoes, Beach Balls	1994	2	5
Disney Collector Series Tumblers	set of eight: Snow White, Jungle Book, Lion King, Peter Pan, Beauty and the Beast, Pinocchio, Dumbo, Aladdin	1994	2	4
Disney Parade Figures	set of four: Mickey, Minnie, Donald, Roger Rabbit	1991	3	5

Rugrats, Burger King, 1998.

Scooby Doo, Burger King, 1996.

! Remember, prices given are for individual pieces only, not complete sets.

Superman, Burger King, 1997.

Teenage Mutant Ninja Turtles
Bike Gear, Burger King, 1993.

Teenage Mutant Ninja Turtles Rad
Badges Insert, Donatello, Burger
King, 1990.

TOY NAME	DESCRIBE	YEAR	EX	MINT
Fairy Tale Cassette Tapes	set of four fairy tale cassettes: Goldilocks, Jack and the Beanstalk, Three Little Pigs, Hansel and Gretel	1989	1	3
Food Miniatures		1983	2	4
Freaky Fellas	set of four: blue, green, red, yellow; each came with a roll of Life Savers candy	1992	1	2
Gargoyles I	set of four: Spin to Life Goliath, Color Mutation Broadway, Gargoyles Pop-up book	1995	1	2
Gargoyles II	set of five: Spectroscope, Sparkling Spinner, Mini-viewer, Spin-attack Broadway, Bronx Launcher	1995	1	2
Go-Go Gadget Gizmos	set of four: Copter Gadget, Inflated Gadget, Scuba Gadget, Surfer Gadget	1992	4	6

Teenage Mutant Ninja Turtles Rad Badges Insert, Heroes on a Halfshell, Burger King, 1990.

Teenage Mutant Ninja Turtles Rad Badges Insert, Leonardo, Burger King, 1990.

! Remember, prices given are for individual pieces only, not complete sets.

Teenage Mutant Ninja Turtles Rad Badges Insert, Michaelangelo, Burger King, 1990.

Teenage Mutant Ninja Turtles Rad Badges Insert, Raphael, Burger King, 1990.

Teenage Mutant Ninja Turtles Rad Badges Insert, Shredder, Burger King, 1990.

TOY NAME	DESCRIBE	YEAR	EX	MINT
Golden Junior Classic Books			1	2
	set of four: Roundabout Train, The Circus Train, Train to Timbucktoo, My Little Book of Trains			
Good Gobblin'		1989	4	8
	set of three: Frankie Steen, Zelda Zoombroom, Gordy Goblin			
Goof Troop Bowlers		1992	3	4
	set of four: Goofy, Pete, PJ Max			
Goofy Movie		1995	2	5
	set of five: Water Raft, Water Skis, Goofy on Bucking Bronco, Row Boat, Runaway Car			
Hunchback of Notre Dame		1996	1	2
	set of eight figures: Laverne, Clopin, Hugo, Frollo, Pheobus, Victor, Quasimodo, Esmerelda and Djali the Goat			

Toonsylvania Insert, Burger King, 1998.

Toonsylvania, Burger King, 1998.

Top Kids, Burger King, 1993.

Universal Monsters, Burger King, 1997.

Watermates, Burger King, 1991.

TOY NAME	DESCRIBE	YEAR	EX	MINT
Hunchback of Notre Dame Puppets four finger: Quasimodo, Esmeralda, Gargoyle, Jester		1996	2	4
It's Magic set of four: Magic Trunk, Disappearing Food, Magic Frame, Remote Control		1992	1	2
Jet Age Meal set of three: Widebody Glider, X-2000 Gilder, Magellan Glider		1982	10	12
Kid's Choice Awards set of six: Slimed Again, Big Bold Blimp, Winning Wiggle Writer, Pop Goes the Rosie, Give the Winner a Hand, Heeeeere's Rosie		1999	1	3
Land Before Time set of six: Littlefoot, Spike, Perle, Chomper, Cera, Duckey		1997	3	6
Lickety Splits set of seven: Carbo Cooler, Carsan'which, Chicken Chassis, Expresstix, Flame Broiled Buggy, Indianapolis Racer, Spry Fries		1990	3	5
Lifesaver Funsters set of four: red, yellow, green, blue		1992	2	4
Lion King Collectible Kingdom set of seven figures: Mufasa, Young Nala, Young Simba, Scar, Rafiki, Ed the Hyena, Pumbaa and Timon		1994	2	3
Lion King Finger Puppets set of six: Mufasa, Simba, Rafiki, Pumbaa and Timon, Ed the Hyena, Scar		1995	1	2
Lion King's Timon & Pumbaa set of four: Timon, Pumbaa, Bug Munchin' Pumbaa, Super Secret Compass		1996	2	3
Little Mermaid Splash Collection set of four: Ariel wind-up, Flounder squirter, Sebastian wind-up, Urchin squirter		1993	2	4
M & M's set of five: red, orange, yellow, blue, green		1997	2	5
M & M's Minis set of five: Chomping Teeth Swarm, Giggle Stick, Crazy Pull-back Swarm, Secret Swarm Squirter, Scoop & Shoot Buggy		1997	1	2

TOY NAME	DESCRIBE	YEAR	EX	MINT
Masters of the Universe Cups	set of four: Thunder Punch He-Man Saves the Day, He-Man and Roboto to the Rescue, He-Man Takes on the Evil Horde, Spydor—Stalking Enemies of Skeletor	1985	3	5
Matchbox Cars	set of four vehicles: blue Mountain Man 4x4, yellow Corvette, red Ferrari, Ford LTD police car	1987	5	7
Men in Black	set of twelve: Squishy Worm Guy, Squirting Worm Guy, Globe Space Spinner, Building Space Spinner, Split Apart Light Up Zed, Split Apart Rotating Zed, Red Button Building Blaster, Red Button Loop Blaster, Slimed Out Kay, Slimed Out Jay, MIB Alien Detector, MIB Neitralyzer	1998	1	3
Mickey's Toontown	set of four: Mickey and Minnie, Goofy, Donald, Chip 'n Dale; each comes with map section	1993	4	7
Mr. Potato Head	set of five: Speedster, Hats Off, Fry Flyer, Spinning Spud, Basket Shoot	1998	1	3
Mr. Potato Head	set of five: Fry Fighter, Gotta Get 'Em Mr. Potato Head, Fry Jumper, Smashed Potato, Light Up Mr. Potato Head	1999	1	3
Nerfuls	set of four: Bitsy Ball, Fetch, Officer Bob, Scratch; rubber characters, interchangeable	1989	5	10
Nickel-O-Zone	set of five: Action League Now, Hay Arnold Football, Alien Strange Pod, Cruising Skeeter, Thornberry Comvee	1998	1	3
Nightmare Before Christmas Wristwatches	set of four different styles		15	30
Oliver & Co.	set of four: Dashing Dodger, Desot Launcher, Skateway Tito, Oliver Viewer; the second Oliver & Co. set was released to coincide with home video release	1996	2	5

TOY NAME	DESCRIBE	YEAR	EX	MINT
Oliver & Company	set of four: Sneak-A-Peek Oliver, Dashing Dodger, Surprise Attack DeSoto, Skateaway Tito	1996	1	2
Pilot Paks	set of four Styrofoam airplanes: two-seater, sunburst, lightning, one unknown example	1988	4	8
Pinocchio Inflatables	set of four: Pinocchio, Jiminy Cricket, Monstro the Whale, Figaro	1992	3	5
Pocahontas Figures	set of eight: Meeko, Governor Radcliffe, Pocahontas, Flit, Captain John Smith, Grandmother Willow, Chief Powhatan, Percy	1995	1	3
Pocahontas Pop-Up Puppets	set of six: Peek-a-Boo Pocahontas, Meeko's Hideout, Pampered Percy, Ruthless Radcliffe, John Smith's Lookout, Busy Body Flit	1996	1	2
Pocahontas Tumblers	set of four: Chief Powhatan, Meeko, Governor Radcliffe, John Smith and Pocahontas	1995	3	5
Purrtenders	set of four: Free Wheeling Cheese Rider, Flip-Top Car, Radio Bank, Storybook	1988	1	3
Purrtenders Plush	set of four: Hop-purr, Flop-purr, Scamp-purr, Romp-purr	1988	2	4
Record Breakers	set of six cars: Aero, Indy, Dominator, Accelerator, Fastland, Shockwave	1990	2	4
Rodney & Friends	set of four plush toys: Rodney, Rhonda, Romona, Randy	1986	2	5
Rodney & Friends Reindeer	Holiday Sweets and Treats, Holiday Fun and Games Box, Holiday Decorating, Holiday at the Toy Store	1987	5	10
Rugrats	set of five: Reptar Alive, Hero on the Move Tommy, Jumpin' Chuckle, Wind Blown Angelica, Tandem Phil & Lil	1998	1	2

! Remember, prices given are for individual pieces only, not complete sets.

TOY NAME	DESCRIBE	YEAR	EX	MINT
Rugrats, The Movie	set of twelve: Okeydokey Tommy, Reptar Wagon, Aqua Reptar, Monkey Mayhem, Phil & Lil: Reptar Mine!, Chuckie's Treasure Hunt, Spike to the Rescue, Shirley Lock Angelica, Dactar Glider, Scooting Susie, Baby Dil Awakened, Clip-On Tommy with Baby Dil	1998	1	2
Save the Animals	set of four: Mammals, Birds, Reptiles and Amphibians, Fish	1993	1	2
Scooby Doo	set of five: Scrappy-Doo, Scooby and Shaggy, Scooby Coffin, Scoby-Doo, Mystery Machine	1996	2	4
Sea Creatures	set of four terrycloth wash mitts: Stella Starfish, Dolly Dolphin, Sammy Seahorse, Ozzie Octopus	1989	2	3
Silverhawks	set of four: Sticker, Name Plate, Decoder Ring, Pencil Topper	1987	5	10
Simpsons cups	set of four	1991	1	2
Simpsons dolls	set of five soft plastic dolls: Bart, Homer, Lisa, Marge, Maggie	1990	2	4
Simpsons figures	set of five each came with cardboard background: Bart with backpack, Homer with skunk, Lisa with saxaphone, Marge with birds, Maggie with turtle	1991	4	8
Small Soldiers	set of twelve: Chip Hazard, Slamfist Soft 'n Cuddly, Rip Roarin' Kip Killigan, Butch's Battle, Bobbling Insaniac, Levitating Lens Ocula, Morning Brake Brick Bazooka, Nick Nitro, Freedom Firing Archer, Laughing Insaniac, Boulder Blasting Punchit & Scratchit, Crawling Link Static	1998	1	3
Spacebase Racers	set of five plastic vehicles: Moon Man Rover, Skylab Cruiser, StarshipViking, Super Shuttle, Cosmic Copter	1989	2	4
Spacebase Racers	set of four: Super Shuttle, Moonman Rover, Starship Viking, Cosmic Copter	1989	5	10

TOY NAME	DESCRIBE	YEAR	EX	MINT
Super Hero Cups	set of four cups with figural handles: Batman, Wonder Woman, Darkseid, Superman	1984	4	10
Super Powers	set of four: Superman coin, Batman toothbrush holder, Aquaman toy, Super Powers door nameplate	1987	7	15
Superman	set of five: Launcher, Phone Booth, Superman, Balancer, Convertible	1997	2	5
Teenage Mutant Ninja Turtles Bike Gear	set of eleven: pouch, horn, water bottle, four spike buttons, three license plates	1993	3	5
Teenage Mutant Ninja Turtles Poster		1991	2	4
Teenage Mutant Ninja Turtles Rad Badges	set of six: Michaelangelo, Leonardo, Raphael, Donatello, Heroes in a Half Shell, Shredder	1990	3	5
Teletubbies	set of six: Laa-Laa, Tinky Winky, Dipsy, Po, Bunny, Noo-Noo	1999	1	3
Thundercats	set of four: cup/bank, Snarf strawholder, light switch plate, secret message ring	1986	3	8
Toonsylvania	set of five: Gurney Getaway, Phil's Teddy Cruiser, Vic's Walkaway Bride, Monster Maker, Screaming Screetch	1998	1	3
Top Kids	set of four spinning tops with figural heads: Wheels, Kid Vid, Jaws, Boomer	1993	1	2
Toy Story	set of six: Hopping Mr. Potato Head, Woody, Action Wing Buzz, Racing R.C. Car, Squash 'N Go Rex, Green Army Men Recon Squad	1995	4	8
Toy Story	set of eight: Stroll 'n Scope Lenny, Jawbreaker Scud, Speedy Deposit Hamm, Round 'em Up Woody, Spin-Top Bo Peep, Blast-away Buzz, Spaced Out Alien, Slinky Dog	1996	2	4

! Remember, prices given are for individual pieces only, not complete sets.

TOY NAME	DESCRIBE	YEAR	EX	MINT
Toy Story Puppets	set of four: Woody, Buzz Lightyear, Rex, Hamm	1995	4	10
Toy Story Talking Puppets	set of four: R.C. Racer, Talking Woody, Talking Buzz	1995	5	12
Tricky Treaters Boxes	Monster Manor, Creepy Castle, Haunted House	1989	1	3
Tricky Treaters Figures	set of three PVC figures: Frankie Steen, Gourdy Goblin, Zelda Zoom Broom	1989	4	10
Trolls Dolls	set of four Kids Club characters with neon hair: Snaps, I/Q Jaws, Kid Vid	1993	1	2
Universal Monsters	set of four: Wolf Man, Frankenstein, Dracula, Creature	1997	4	8
Watermates	set of four: Lingo's Jet Ski, Snaps in Boat, Wheels on raft, I/Q on dolphin	1991	1	2
Wild Wild West		1999	1	2
Z-bots	set of five: Bugeye, Buzzsaw, Jawbreaker, Skyviper, Turbine	1994	1	2

Boxes

Airplane	yellow, smiling	1988	7	10
Airplane	red, propeller	1988	7	10
Animal Boxes	set of four activity booklets: bear, hippo, lion, one unknown box	1986	1	2
Bone Age Meal Pack	Prehistoric Creatures are Wonderful Teachers	1989	7	10
Bone Age Meal Pack	The Greatest Mystery in History	1989	7	10

TOY NAME	DESCRIBE	YEAR	EX	MINT
Bone Age Skeleton Kit		1989	1	2
	The Past is a Blast, The Greatest Mystery in History, Zap Back to the Bone Age, Prehistoric Creatures are Wonderful Teachers			
Dino Meals	red	1987	7	10
Dino Meals	purple	1987	7	10
Meal Bots	gold and purple	1986	8	15
Meal Bots	silver and green	1986	8	15
Meal Bots	red and pink	1986	8	15

Airplane, Burger King, 1988.

Airplane, Burger King, 1988.

! Remember, prices given are for individual pieces only, not complete sets.

Bone Age Meal Pack, Burger King, 1989.

Dino Meals, Burger King, 1987.

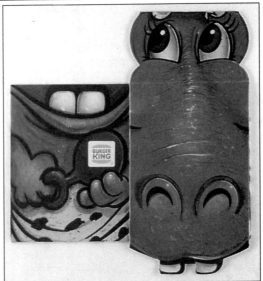

Dino Meals, Burger King, 1987.

TOY NAME	DESCRIBE	YEAR	EX	MINT
Meal Bots	silver and blue	1986	8	15
Purrtenders	The Escapades		8	15
Super Powers Meal Pack			5	10
The Adventures of Alf on Melmac	The Many Faces of Alf: "Melmac Girls" record; available with the purchase of five plush Alf toys from Coleco	1987	2	4
The Adventures of Alf on Melmac	The Many Faces of Alf: "Take Me, Alf, to the Ballgame" record; available with the purchase of five plush Alf toys from Coleco	1987	2	4
The Chipmunk Adventure Meal	shows The Chipmunks and Chipettes being chased through an airport	1987	8	15
The Chipmunk Adventure Meal	While in Mexico, the Chipmunks visit an old town square	1987	8	15

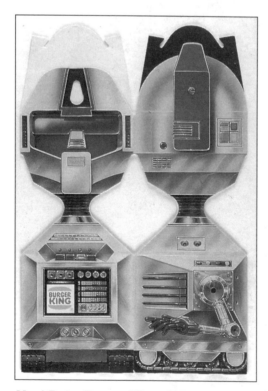

Meal Bots, Burger King, 1986.

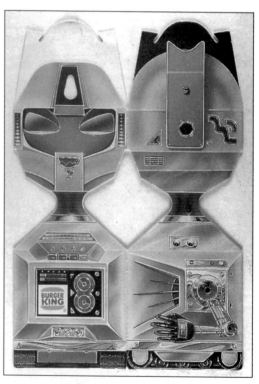

Meal Bots, Burger King, 1986.

! Remember, prices given are for individual pieces only, not complete sets.

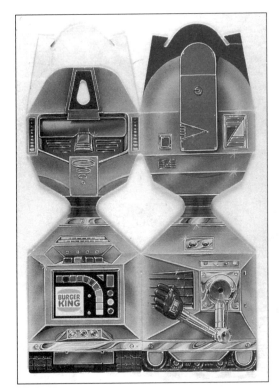

Meal Bots, Burger King, 1986.

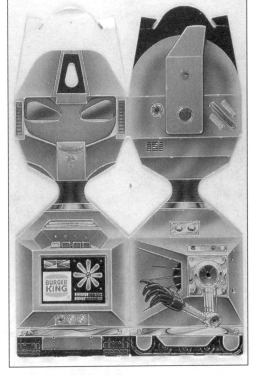

Meal Bots, Burger King, 1986.

Purrtenders, Burger King.

TOY NAME	DESCRIBE	YEAR	EX	MINT
The Get Along Gang		1985	8	15
Thundercats		1986	10	18
	Thundercats on Patrol			
Train			3	6
	blue with hippo			
Train			3	6
	green with hippo			

Super Powers Meal Pack (front), Burger King.

Super Powers Meal Pack (back), Burger King.

! Remember, prices given are for individual pieces only, not complete sets.

The Adventures of Alf on Melmac, Burger King, 1987.

The Adventures of Alf on Melmac: "Take Me, Alf, to the Ballgame" record (front), Burger King, 1987.

The Adventures of Alf on Melmac: "Take Me, Alf, to the Ballgame" record (back), Burger King, 1987.

The Chipmunk Adventure Meal, Burger King, 1987.

The Chipmunk Adventure Meal, Burger King, 1987.

! Remember, prices given are for individual pieces only, not complete sets.

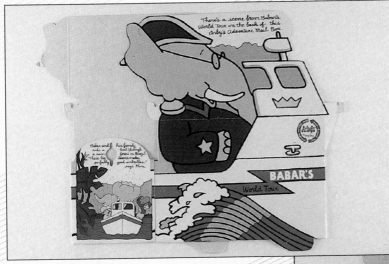

Babar's World Tour
Adventure Meal Box 14
(front), Arby's, 1991.

Babar's World Tour
Adventure Meal Box 14
(back), Arby's, 1991.

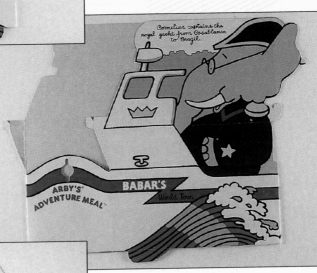

Triple Play Funmeal Boxes,
Burger Chef, 1978.
Photo courtesy Museum of
Science and Industry, Chicago

Village Funmeal Boxes,
Burger Chef, 1975.
Photo courtesy Museum of
Science and Industry, Chicago.

Star Wars Funmeal Boxes,
Burger Chef, 1978.
Photo courtesy Museum of
Science and Industry, Chicago.

Fun 'n Games Booklet, Burger Chef.
Photo courtesy Museum of Science
and Industry, Chicago.

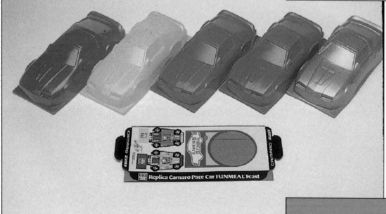

Race Cars, Burger Chef, 1981.
Photo courtesy Museum of
Science and Industry, Chicago.

Cartoon Network Racing
Team, Burger King, 1997.

Pocahontas Pop-Up Puppets,
Burger King, 1996.
Photo courtesy Burger King.

Toy Story Puppets, Burger King,
1995. Photo courtesy Burger King.

BK Kids Club Glo-Force,
Burger King, 1996.
Photo courtesy Burger King.

BK Kids Club Coolers,
Burger King, 1995.
Photo courtesy Burger King.

BK Kids Club Planet Patrol,
Burger King, 1997.

Speed Bunnies, Hardee's, 1994.
Photo courtesy Museum of
Science and Industry, Chicago.

Little Golden Books Meal:
The Little Red Caboose (front),
Hardee's, 1988.

Little Golden Books Meal:
The Little Red Caboose
(back), Hardee's, 1988.

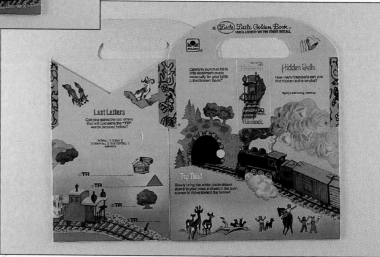

**Extreme Ghostbusters,
Kentucky Fried Chicken,
1997.**

**Sea Walkers,
Long John Silver's, 1990.
Photo courtesy Museum of
Science and Industry, Chicago.**

**Air Garfield, Paratrooper,
Pizza Hut, 1993.
Photo courtesy Museum of
Science and Industry, Chicago.**

**Young Indiana Jones Chronicles,
Pizza Hut, 1993.
Photo courtesy Museum of
Science and Industry, Chicago.**

Furby, McDonald's, 1999.

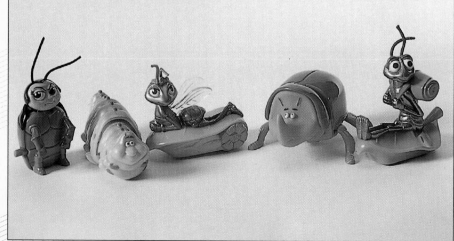

Recess, McDonald's, 1998.

Space Jam,
McDonald's, 1996.

A Bug's Life,
McDonald's,
1998.

Teenie Beanie
Babies,
McDonald's, 1998.

Fun with Food, McDonald's, 1989.

Peanuts, Canadian,
McDonald's, 1989.
Photo courtesy Museum of
Science and Industry, Chicago.

Alvin and The Chipmunks,
McDonald's, 1991.
Photo courtesy Museum of
Science and Industry, Chicago.

Astrosnicks I, McDonald's, 1983.
Photo courtesy Museum of
Science and Industry, Chicago.

Barbie and Friends/World of Hot Wheels, McDonald's, 1994. Photo courtesy Museum of Science and Industry, Chicago.

Cabbage Patch Kids/Tonka, McDonald's, 1992. Photo courtesy Museum of Science and Industry, Chicago.

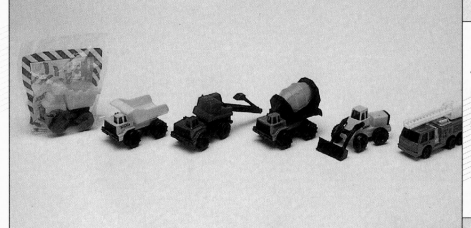

Tonka/Cabbage Patch Kids, McDonald's, 1992. Photo courtesy Museum of Science and Industry, Chicago.

Dink the Little Dinosaur, McDonald's, 1990. Photo courtesy Museum of Science and Industry, Chicago.

Disney Masterpiece Collection, McDonald's, 1996. Photo courtesy Museum of Science and Industry, Chicago.

Flintstone Kids, McDonald's, 1988. Photo courtesy Museum of Science and Industry, Chicago.

Michael Jordan Fitness Fun Challenge, McDonald's, 1992. Photo courtesy Museum of Science and Industry, Chicago.

Ronald McDonald Celebrates Happy Birthday, McDonald's, 1994. Photo courtesy Museum of Science and Industry, Chicago.

Jungle Book, McDonald's, 1990.
Photo courtesy Museum of
Science and Industry, Chicago.

Kissyfur, McDonald's, 1987.
Photo courtesy Museum of
Science and Industry, Chicago.

Mac Tonight, McDonald's, 1988.
Photo courtesy Museum of
Science and Industry, Chicago.

Mickey and Friends
Epcot Center '94 Adventure,
McDonald's, 1994.
Photo courtesy Museum of
Science and Industry, Chicago.

**Mickey's Birthdayland,
McDonald's, 1989.
Photo courtesy Museum of
Science and Industry, Chicago.**

**Transformers/My Little Pony,
McDonald's, 1985.
Photo courtesy Museum of
Science and Industry, Chicago.**

**101 Dalmatians,
McDonald's, 1991.
Photo courtesy Museum of
Science and Industry, Chicago.**

**Potato Head Kids II,
McDonald's, 1992.
Photo courtesy Museum of
Science and Industry, Chicago.**

Snow White and the Seven Dwarfs, McDonald's, 1993. Photo courtesy Museum of Science and Industry, Chicago.

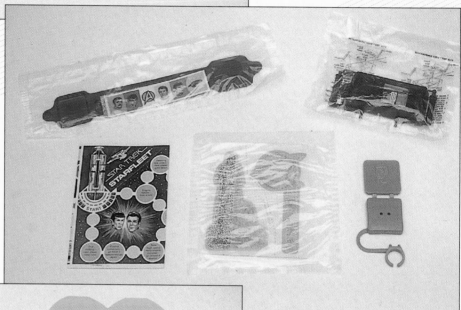

Star Trek, McDonald's, 1979. Photo courtesy Museum of Science and Industry, Chicago.

Healing through Happiness, McDonald's, 1995. Photo courtesy Museum of Science and Industry, Chicago.

Teenie Beanie Babies International Bears, McDonlad's, 1999.

Be a Sport: Bicycle Kick, Pitcher, (back), Roy Rogers, 1989.

Be a Sport: Jump Shot, Angle Block (front), Roy Rogers, 1989.

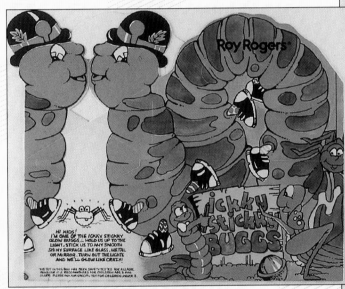

Ickky Stickky Buggs: orange and brown caterpillar (front), Roy Rogers, 1987.

Ickky Stickky Buggs: orange and brown caterpillar (back), Roy Rogers, 1987.

Gator Tales, Roy Rogers, 1989.
Photo courtesy Museum of
Science and Industry, Chicago.

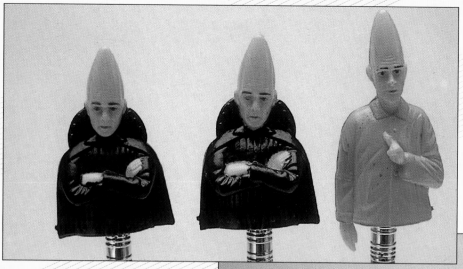

Conehead Pencil Toppers,
Subway, 1993.
Photo courtesy Museum of
Science and Industry, Chicago.

Santa Claus, Subway, 1994.
Photo courtesy Museum of
Science and Industry, Chicago.

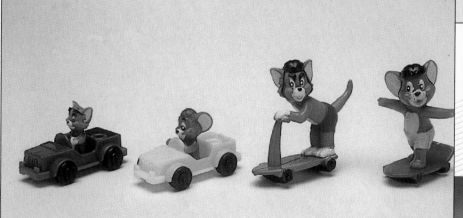

Tom and Jerry, Subway, 1994.
Photo courtesy Museum of
Science and Industry, Chicago.

Blues Clues, Subway, 1998.
Photo courtesy Subway.

Alf Tales, Wendy's, 1990.

**Jetsons Figures, Wendy's, 1989.
Photo courtesy Museum of
Science and Industry, Chicago.**

**Mighty Mouse, Wendy's, 1989.
Photo courtesy Museum of
Science and Industry, Chicago.**

**Teddy Ruxpin, Wendy's, 1987.
Photo courtesy Museum of
Science and Industry, Chicago.**

Wacky Wind-Ups, Wendy's, 1991. Photo courtesy Museum of Science and Industry, Chicago.

Yogi Bear and Friends, Wendy's, 1990. Photo courtesy Museum of Science and Industry, Chicago.

Castle Meal Family, White Castle, 1992. Photo courtesy Museum of Science and Industry, Chicago.

Fat Albert and the Cosby Kids, White Castle, 1990. Photo courtesy Museum of Science and Industry, Chicago.

The Get Along Gang (front), Burger King, 1985.

The Get Along Gang (back), Burger King, 1985.

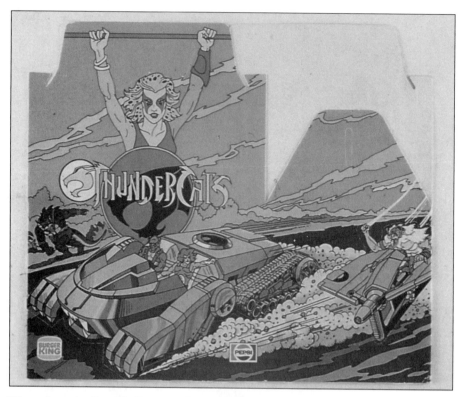

Thundercats (front), Burger King, 1986.

Thundercats (back), Burger King, 1986.

❗ Remember, prices given are for individual pieces only, not complete sets.

Train, Burger King.

Train, Burger King.

Hardee's

Wilbur Hardee opened his first drive-in restaurant in Greenville, North Carolina, in the fall of 1960 and immediately attracted the attention of Leonard Walls, Jr. and Jim Gardner, two Rocky Mount, North Carolina businessmen. Impressed by Hardee's success, Walls and Gardner joined him in his endeavor and created Hardee's Drive-Ins, and in 1961, they opened their first company-owned restaurant in Rocky Mount. Today, Hardee's Food Systems, Inc, a wholly-owned subsidiary of CKE Restaurants, Inc., owns and operates 2,900 restaurants in thirty-four states and eleven countries.

Although Hardee's has been offering kid's meal premiums since the early 1980s, their California Raisins promotion from 1987 was one of their most successful. Based on the popular advertising campaign by the California Raisin Advisory Board, over fifty million raisin items were sold. The Smurfs promotion of 1987 was a collector's dream with over 100 of the little blue characters available. Without a master list of all the Smurfs issued, collectors can spend years trying to compile an entire set.

Hardee's continues to produce toys but hasn't been able to meet the success they had with some of their previous promotions.

TOY NAME	DESCRIBE	YEAR	EX	MINT
Apollo 13		1995	2	5
Beach Bunnies	set of four: girl with ball, boy with skateboard, girl with skates, boy with frisbee	1989	2	4
California Raisins	set of four: dancer with blue and white shoes, singer with mike, sax player, raisin with sunglasses	1987	2	4
California Raisins	set of six: Waves Weaver, F.F. Strings, Captain Toonz, Rollin' Rollo, Trumpy Tru-Note, S.B. Stuntz	1988	2	4
California Raisins	set of four: Berry, Anita Break, Alotta Stile, Buster	1991	3	5
California Raisins	set of four: Alotta Stile in pink boots, Anita Break with package under her arm, Benny bowling, Buster with skateboard	1991	3	7
California Raisins Plush	set of four: lady in yellow shoes, dancer in yellow hat, with mike in white shoes, in sunglasses with orange hat; each 6" tall	1988	2	4

! Remember, prices given are for individual pieces only, not complete sets.

California Raisins, Hardee's, 1987 and 1988. Photo courtesy Museum of Science and Industry, Chicago.

California Raisins, Hardee's, 1991.

Days of Thunder Racers Insert, Hardee's, 1990.

TOY NAME	DESCRIBE	YEAR	EX	MINT
Camp California	set of four: Bear Squirter, Lil' Bro Disk, Mini Volleyball, Spinner; similar to set issued by Carl's Jr.	1993	2	5
Days of Thunder Racers	set of four cars: Mello Yello #51, Hardee's #18 orange, City Chevrolet #46, Superflo #46 pink/white	1990	2	4
Dinosaur in My Pocket	set of four: Stegosaurus, Triceratops, Bronotsaurus, Tyrannosaurus	1993	2	4
Disney's Animated Classics Plush Toys	Pinocchio, Bambi		3	4
Fender Bender 500	set of five: Yogi and Boo Boo, Huckleberry Hound and Snagglepuss, Magilla Gorilla and Wally Gator, Quick Draw McGraw and Baba Looey, Dick Dasterdly and Muttley; also issued by Carl's Jr.	1990	2	3
Finger Crayons	set of four: two Crayons included in each package; not marked Hardee's	1992	2	4

Flintstones First 30 Years, Hardee's, 1991. Photo courtesy Museum of Science and Industry, Chicago.

Food Squirters, Hardee's, 1990. Photo courtesy Museum of Science and Industry, Chicago.

! Remember, prices given are for individual pieces only, not complete sets.

Ghostbusters Beepers, Hardee's, 1989. Photo courtesy Museum of Science and Industry, Chicago.

Homeward Bound, Hardee's.

Marvel Super Heroes, Hardee's, 1990. Photo courtesy Museum of Science and Industry, Chicago.

TOY NAME	DESCRIBE	YEAR	EX	MINT
Flintstones First 30 Years		1991	3	7
	set of five: Fred with TV, Barney with grill, Pebbles with phone, Dino with jukebox, Bamm Bamm with pinball			
Food Squirters		1990	2	4
	set of four: cheeseburger, hot dog, shake, fries			
Food Squirters		1990	3	5
	set of four neon squirters: cheeseburger, hot dog, shake, fries			
Ghostbuster Beepers		1989	10	15
	set of four: red, white, black, gray			
Gremlin Adventures		1989	2	4
	set of five book and record sets: Gift of the Mogwai, Gismo & the Gremlins, Escape from the Gremlins, Gremlins Trapped, The Late Gremlin			
Halloween Hideaways		1989	3	6
	set of four: goblin in blue cauldron, ghost in yellow bag, cat in pumpkin, bat in stump			

COME SURF WITH **SMURF**®
AT **HARDEE'S**®!

COLLECT ALL 6 SURFIN' SMURFS®

Smurfin' Smurfs Insert, front, Hardee's, 1990.

Smurfin' Smurfs Insert, back, Hardee's, 1990.

ALL SIX SMURFIN' SMURFS ®
AVAILABLE EXCLUSIVELY
AT PARTICIPATING
HARDEE'S®
RESTAURANTS
WHILE SUPPLIES LAST
SMURF®   © *Peyo*
LICENSED BY APPLAUSE LICENSING

SAFE FOR CHILDREN OF ALL **AGES**
SEE DETAILS AT STORE

! Remember, prices given are for individual pieces only, not complete sets.

TOY NAME	DESCRIBE	YEAR	EX	MINT
Hardee's Racer	blue or green		2	4
Home Alone 2	set of four cups: Kevin, The Pigeo Lady, Marv, Harry	1992	1	2
Homeward Bound	set of five: Chance, Riley, Sassy, Delilah, Shadow		2	4
Kazoo Crew Sailors	set of four: bear, monkey, rabbit, rhino	1991	2	3
Little Little Golden Books	set of four: The Poky Little Puppy, Little Red Riding Hood, The Three Little Pigs, The Little Red Hen	1987	2	4
Little Little Golden Books	set of four: The Little Red Caboose, The Three Bears, Old MacDonald Had a Farm, Three Little Kittens	1988	2	4
Marvel Super Heroes	set of three: She Hulk, Hulk, Captain America, Spider-Man	1990	3	6
Muppet Christmas Carol Finger Puppets	set of four: Miss Piggy, Kermit, Gonzo, Fozzy Bear	1994	3	5
Nicktoons	set of eight: Ren, Stimpy, Angelica Pickles, Tommy Pickles, Porkchop, Doug Funnie, Rocko, Spunky	1994	1	2
Pound Puppies	set of four: black, white with black, tan with black, gray with black	1986	5	10
Pound Puppies and Pur-r-ries	set of four: white cat with gray stripes, brown cat, gray bulldog, Damlatian	1987	5	10
Ren & Stimpy		1994	1	3
Shirt Tales Plush Dolls	set of five: Bogey, Pammy, Tyg, Digger, Rick; each 7" tall		2	4
Smurfin' Smurfs	set of four: Papa Smurf with red board, Smurf with orange board, Smurfette with purple board, dog with blue board, Smurfette on green board	1990	5	9

TOY NAME	DESCRIBE	YEAR	EX	MINT
Smurfs figures	Hardee's issued over 100 Smurfs in the promotion; no list is available	1987	2	4
Speed Bunnies	set of four: Cruiser, Dusty, Sunny, Stretch	1994	2	4
Super Bowl Cloisonné Pins	set of twenty-five NFL Super Bowl pins	1991	2	6
Swan Princess	set of four: Prince Derek, Princess Odette/Swan, Jean-Bob, Puffin, Rothbart	1994	2	4
Tang Mouth Figures	set of four: Lance, Tag, Flap, Awesome Annie	1989	2	4
Waldo and Friends Holiday Ornaments	came in sets of three: Waldo with Woof, Waldo Watchers, Snowman; Waldo with camping gear, Wenda, Woof; Reindeer in sleigh, Wizard, Waldo with books	1991	2	4
Waldo's Straw Buddies	set of four: Waldo, Wenda, Wizard, Woof	1990	2	3
Waldo's Travel Adventure	set of four: Adventure Travel Journal, Postcards, Fold 'N Solve Travel Pictures, Space Puzzle	1992	2	3
X-Men	came in sets of two: Cyclops vs. Commando, Phantasia vs. Storm, The Blob vs. Wolverine, Rogue vs. Wolverine	1995	3	6

Waldo's Straw Buddies, Hardee's, 1990. Photo courtesy Museum of Science and Industry, Chicago.

! Remember, prices given are for individual pieces only, not complete sets.

TOY NAME	DESCRIBE	YEAR	EX	MINT
Boxes				
Days of Thunder Funmeal Pack		1990	5	10
Little Golden Books Meal	Old MacDonald Had a Farm	1988	5	10
Little Golden Books Meal	The Little Red Caboose	1988	5	10
Little Golden Books Meal	The Three Bears	1988	5	10
Pound Puppies Children's Meals	The Mountain Cabin	1987	8	15
Pound Puppies Children's Meals	The Country Cabin	1987	8	15
Pound Puppies Children's Meals	The Townhouse	1987	8	15

Days of Thunder Funmeal Pack (front), Hardee's, 1990.

Days of Thunder Funmeal Pack (back), Hardee's, 1990.

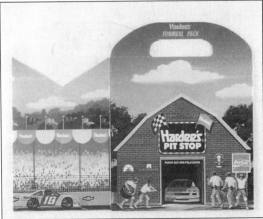

TOY NAME	DESCRIBE	YEAR	EX	MINT
Pound Puppies Children's Meals The Beach House		1987	8	15
Smurfs		1987	5	10
	Smurf Angle, Stop & Smurf the Flowers, Smurfy Tongue Twisters, Smurf Away; used in first Smurf promotion, window in box showed which Smurf was featured in the meal.			
Squirters Children's Meal		1990	4	8

Little Golden Books Meal: Old MacDonald Had a Farm (front), Hardee's, 1988.

Little Golden Books Meal: Old MacDonald Had a Farm (back), Hardee's, 1988.

Little Golden Books Meal: The Three Bears (front), Hardee's, 1988.

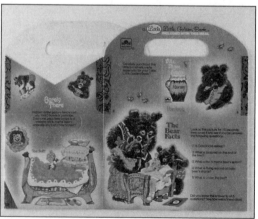

Little Golden Books Meal: The Three Bears (back), Hardee's, 1988.

! Remember, prices given are for individual pieces only, not complete sets.

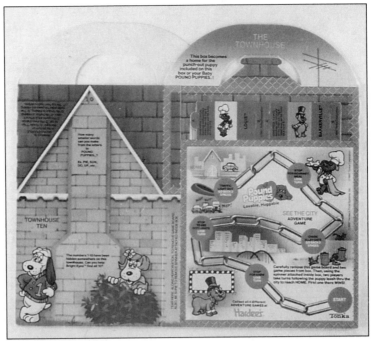

Pound Puppies Children's Meals (back), Hardee's, 1987.

Pound Puppies Children's Meals: The Beach House (front), Hardee's, 1987.

Pound Puppies Children's Meals: The Beach House (back), Hardee's, 1987.

Pound Puppies Children's Meals: The Country Cabin (front), Hardee's, 1987.

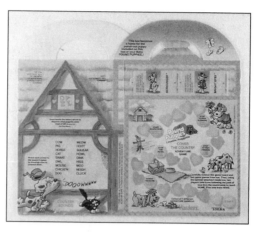

Pound Puppies Children's Meals: The Country Cabin (back), Hardee's, 1987.

Pound Puppies Children's Meals: The Mountain Cabin (front), Hardee's, 1987.

Pound Puppies Children's Meals: The Mountain Cabin (back), Hardee's, 1987.

Squirters Children's Meal (back), Hardee's, 1990.

Squirters Children's Meal (front), Hardee's, 1990.

! Remember, prices given are for individual pieces only, not complete sets.

KFC

Colonel Harland Sanders founded KFC in 1952, and began actively franchising his Original Recipe chicken in 1956 when he was sixty-six years old and living on a $100 Social Security check. The colonel traveled the country by car preparing his chicken for restaurant owners. If they liked it, he let them use his secret blend of eleven herbs and spices under the agreement that they pay him five cents for every chicken sold. Colonel Sanders had over 600 franchised outlets when he sold his interest in the company for $2 million in 1964. He remained the spokesman for the company until his death in 1980.

Kentucky Fried Chicken and Colonel Sanders have become American icons. Millions of people have fond memories of eating fried chicken out of a red-and-white striped bucket. KFC has recently revived Colonel Sanders in advertising featuring an animated Colonel, and in 1996 brought back the bucket.

KFC jumped into the kid's meal race in 1996 with its Garfield promotion. Since they have other popular promotions of Pokémon and *Star Wars: Episode I The Phantom Menace*. The *Star Wars* toys, done together with Pizza Hut and Taco Bell, was well done and well marketed. The quality of the toys together with the subject of Star Wars will help ensure that this promotion will hold up well in the world of collectibles.

TOY NAME	DESCRIBE	YEAR	EX	MINT
Alvin and the Chipmunks Canadian issues; Alvin and Theodore		1991	3	5
Alvin and the Chipmunks Canadian issues; Alvin and Simon		1992	2	4
Animorphs set of five: Animorphs Puzzle Cube, DNA Transfer Cards, Animorphing Box, Tobias Hawk Glider, Thought Speak Revealer		1998	2	3
Beakman's World set of six: Lester Reverser, Penguin TV, Optical Illusion Top, Diver Don, Beakman's Balancer, Dancing Liza		1998	2	3
Carmen Sandiego set of six: Jr. Sleuth Pocket Pack, Carmen's Mystery Decoder, Carmen's World Map Puzzle, Carmen's Breakaway Escape Care, Carmen's Undercover Case with Stickers, Magic Answer Globe		1997	2	3
Colonel Sanders Figure 9" tall		1960s	35	50
Colonel Sanders Nodder 7" tall; plastic		1960s	15	40
Colonel Sanders Nodder 7" tall; papier-mâché		1960s	50	150

TOY NAME	DESCRIBE	YEAR	EX	MINT
Cool Summer Stuff featuring Chester Cheetah set of five: Fast Flyin' Disk, Spotted Summer Shades, Mini Wrist-Pack, Totally Fun Visor, Inflatable Wobble Ball		1996	1	2
Extreme Ghostbusters set of six: Haunted Cube, Ghost Trap Challenge, Screamin' Scrambler, Ecto1 Haunted Hauler, Ghostbusters Keychain Keeper, Slimer Squirter		1997	2	3
Garfield Catmobiles set of six: Arlene finger puppet, Pookie finger puppet, Nermal Freewheeler, Jon Freewheeler, Garfield Pullback, Odie Pullback		1996	2	3
Garfield Racers set of six		1996	2	4
Ghostly Glowing Squirters set of six: Casper, Spooky, Stretch, Fatso, Poil, Stinkie		1996	2	3

Animorphs, KFC, 1998.

! Remember, prices given are for individual pieces only, not complete sets.

Beakman's World, KFC, 1998.

Extreme Ghostbusters Insert, KFC, 1998.

Pokémon Insert, KFC, 1999.

TOY NAME	DESCRIBE	YEAR	EX	MINT
Giga Pets	set of four: Digipooch, Cyberkitty, Micropup, Bitty Kitty; over the counter promotion	1997	2	3
Jim Henson's Scary Scary Monsters	set of five: Flip-A-Mungo, Super Stretch Norbert, Zuzu Zoomer, Monster Shoelace Munchers, Scary Scary Stick-Ons	2000	2	3
Koosh	set of three: Zipper Pull, Bookmark, Pencil Topper	1995	1	2
Linkbots	set of six Transformers	1995	2	3
Marvel Super Heroes	set of six: Spider-Man Symbol Clip, Invisible Woman Escape Launcher, Incredible Hulk Pencil Twirler, Spider-Man Wall Walker, Fantastic Four Terra Craft, Wolverine Press 'n Go	1997	1	2
Masked Rider to the Rescue	set of six: Masked Rider Super Gold, Magno the Super Car, Press & Go Super Chopper, Glow-in-the-Dark X-Ray Cyclopter, Ecto Viewer Wrist Band, Bump & Go Ferbus	1997	1	2

Pokémon, KFC, 1998.

! Remember, prices given are for individual pieces only, not complete sets.

Secret Files of the Spy Dogs, KFC, 1999.

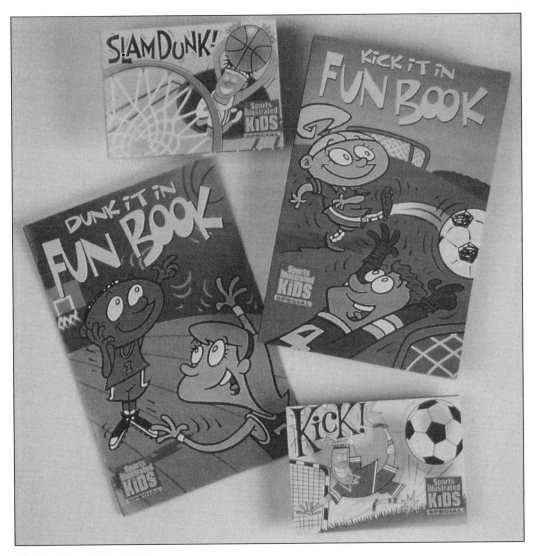

SI for Kids, KFC, 1998.

TOY NAME	DESCRIBE	YEAR	EX	MINT
Matchbox	set of six: BMW, Ambulance, Fire Engine, Mustang, Jeep, Ferrari	1995	2	3
NCAA March Madness	set of three: 2-Hoop Game, Wacky Wrist Toss, Final Four Basketball	1999	2	3
Pokémon	set of six: Pokémon Monster Blocks, Go Pokémon Card Game, Pokémon Monster Matcher, Pokémon Tattoos, Ivysaur Squirter, Pikachu Treasure Keeper	1998	2	3
Pokémon Beanbags	set of four: Seel, Vulpix, Dratini, Zubat; over-the-counter promotion	1998	2	5
Secret Files of the Spy Dogs	set of five: The Evil Cat Astrophe, Fidgety Scribble, Mitzy Rolling Stamper, Eye Popping Space Slug, Agent Ralph's Marble Game	1999	1	2

Slimamander, KFC, 1998.

! Remember, prices given are for individual pieces only, not complete sets.

Wallace & Gromit, KFC, 1998.

Winter Wonderpals, KFC, 1999.

TOY NAME	DESCRIBE	YEAR	EX	MINT
SI for Kids	set of four: Dunk It In Fun Book, Slam Dunk! Flipbook, Kick it in Fun Book, Kick! Flipbook	1998	1	2
Slimamander	set of six: Slimamander Wrist Squirter, Slimamander's Glowing Goo, Slimamander and Leap the Frog Tattoos, Leap the Frog Launcher, Slimamander Bubble Wand, Slimamander Spraying Top	1998	1	2
Star Wars Episode I, The Phantom Menace: Cup Toppers	set of four: Queen Amidala, Captain Tarpals, Boss Nass, R2D2; over-the-counter promotion sold for $2.99 with food purchase	1999	2	3
Star Wars Episode I, The Phantom Menace: Flying Bucket Toppers	set of two: Jar Jar Binks, Battle Droid; over-the-counter promotion sold over the counter for $1.99	1999	2	3
Star Wars Episode I, The Phantom Menace	set of ten: Jar Jar Binks Squirter, Queen Amidala's Hidden Identity, Anakin Skywalker's Naboo Fighter, Trade Federation Droid Fighter, Planet Naboo, Swimming Jar Jar Binks, Opee Sea Creature Chaser, Naboo Ground Battle, Gungan Sub Squirter, Boss Nass Squirter	1999	3	5
Timon and Pumbaa's World of Bugs	set of six: Snail Snackin' Timon, Bug Munchin' Pumbaa, Out-to-Lunch Timon, Hawaiian Luau Pumbaa, Jungle River-Riding Timon, Bug Bath Pumbaa	1997	2	3
Treeples	set of six: Dress-Up Rachel, Stevie's Acorn Searcher, Tangled Treeples, Othello Yo-Yo, Miranda's Banana-mated Theater, Linky Lurker	2000	1	2
Ultimate Eekstravaganza	set of five: Eek! Balancing Act, Sharky's Dog House Launcher, Ka-Boooom! Annabelle, Cool Moves Doc, Kutler Copter	1996	2	3

! Remember, prices given are for individual pieces only, not complete sets.

TOY NAME	DESCRIBE	YEAR	EX	MINT
Wallace & Gromit set of six: The Wrong Trousers, Gromit's Rollalong Sidecar, Wallace Bendable, Wallace & Gromit Character Card Set, Sheep-on-a-String, Blinking Feathers McGraw		1998	2	3
Winter Wonderpals set of five: Wallace the Walrus Paper Puncher, Roley Poley Polar Ball, Sippy the Penguin Play Straw, Slick the Sled Dog Igloo Launcher, Howl E. Wolf		1999	2	3
WWF Stampers set of four: Canadian issues			2	4

Long John Silver's

Long John Silver's began in 1969 as Long John Silver's Fish 'n' Chips. Named after a character in Robert Louis Stevenson's classic, *Treasure Island*, they have grown to become America's largest fast food seafood chain with over 1,300 located in thirty-five states.

Long before the first kid's meal was served, Long John Silver's offered toys to youngsters. Children were given a token they could use to "buy" a small toy. Although there are some premiums dating back to the 1980s, such as the Fish Cars from 1986, they didn't venture into the more traditional kid's meal until the early 1990s.

The Sea Walkers, offered in 1990, consisted of a Parrot, Penguin, Turtle and Sylvia walkers with attached coins. Difficult to find with the coin, they are valued $8 in Mint condition.

Long John Silver's has yet to produce a promotion of great substance, this is despite securing the license for popular characters like the Muppets and the Peanuts gang. This is due to low distribution and low quality of their promotions.

TOY NAME	DESCRIBE	YEAR	EX	MINT
Adventure on Volcano Island	paint with water activity book	1991	2	4
Berenstain Bear books		1995	2	5
Bobby's World	set of seven: Play Clay (2), Silly Straw (2), Eye Viewer (2), License Plate	1999	1	3
Dinoworld	set of six: dinosaur figures (4), fossil stencil gate, game sheet	1997	1	3
Disney Channel		1997	2	4
Fish Cars	fish-shaped cars done in red, yellow and blue, each with different peel-off stickers and details	1986	8	12
Garfield in Space		1998	2	4
Joe Cool Secret Agent Mystery Series	set of four: camera, telescope, watch, whistle	1997	1	3
Kitty in my Pocket	set of six: Magnetic, Fantasy, Orient, Miky, Aimee, Lauren	1996	1	3

! Remember, prices given are for individual pieces only, not complete sets.

Kitty in My Pocket, Long John Silver's, 1996.

Life with Louie, Long John Silver's, 1999.

TOY NAME	DESCRIBE	YEAR	EX	MINT
Life with Louie	set of seven: Sidewalk Chalk (2), Spinner Darts (2), Sercet Stuff Wrist Band, "Bully" Balls (2)	1999	1	3
Lost in Space		1998	2	4
Magic School Bus	set of four: Dump Truck Bus, Fire Truck Buss, Balancing Building Buss, Maraca and Horn	1997	1	3
Mega Blocks		1998	1	3
Oliver Twist	set of eight: Switch-a-Pic Buildings (2), Twist Character Blocks (2), Twist-a-Story Coloring Roll (2), Sticker Tote book	1997	1	3
Once Upon a Forest	set of five straw huggers: Abigail, Michelle, Cornelius, Edgar, Russell; done in two mold colors	1993	3	6
Peanuts Easter		1997	2	4
Pound Puppies	set of eight puppies with adoption certificates	1996	2	4

Oliver Twist, Long John Silver's, 1997.

! Remember, prices given are for individual pieces only, not complete sets.

Princess Gwenevere, Long John Silver's, 1996.

Skysurfers, Long John Silver's, 1996.

TOY NAME	DESCRIBE	YEAR	EX	MINT
Princess Gwenevere	set of four figures: Princess Gwenevere, Sunstar her horse, Archie the owl, Spike the panther	1996	1	3
School House Rocks		1998	2	4
Sea Goggles		1996	1	3
Sea Walkers	set of four packaged with string: Parrot, Penguin, Turtle, Sylvia	1990	3	8
Sea Watchers Kaleidoscopes	set of three: orange, yellow, pink	1991	2	4
Skysurfers	set of four figures: Crazy Stunts, Cyclone, Sky/Surfer One, Skyboard	1996	1	3
Space Goofs	set of five: Fun Flyer (2), Glow-in-the-Dark Light Switch Cover, Bio-Dome, Playing Cards	1999	1	3
Superstar Baseball Cards	eight sets of five cards: Don Mattingly, Mark McGwire, Mark Grace, Wade Boggs, Darryl Strawberry, Nolan Ryan, Bobby Bonilla, Bret Saberhagen	1990	10	15

Winter Muppetland, Long John Silver's, 1998.

! Remember, prices given are for individual pieces only, not complete sets.

TOY NAME	DESCRIBE	YEAR	EX	MINT
Treasure Trolls	set of six: yellow hair, red hair, pink hair, blue hair, purple hair, green hair	1992	1	3
Water Blasters	set of four: Billy Bones, Captain Flint, Ophelia Octopus, Parrot	1990	3	5
Winter Muppetland	set of four: Miss Piggy, Kermit the Frog, Fozzie Bear, Gonzo the Great	1998	2	4

McDonald's

McDonald's is the undisputed king of the fast food world. Dick and Mac McDonald were the proprietors of the first McDonald's in San Bernardino, California, and it was in 1954 when Ray Kroc, distributor of the Multimixer, heard of a restaurant in California running eight Multimixers at once. Impressed by the number of people they could serve at one time, Kroc suggested to the McDonald brothers that they open more restaurants. (Kroc was also thinking about how many Multimixers he could sell to each store.) The following year, Kroc opened the second McDonald's in Des Plaines, Illinois.

The face of the American city began to change during the 1950s. Young families were abandoning the urban centers to raise their families in the suburbs. The car was king. The youngest members of the baby boom turned seven in 1955. McDonald's appealed to every aspect of the new face of the American family. Unlike other fast food chains, McDonald's were located in the growing suburbs, and they quickly became the ideal place for the youn'g adult to show off his new car and for the young father to show off his family. From the beginning, with it's spokesperson, Ronald McDonald, and inexpensive burgers, McDonald's appealed to the younger generation.

The 1970s were a time for growth and growing pains for America's favorite burger chain. McDonaldland was created in 1970 to reach out to the youth of America by creating a cast of characters—Mayor McCheese, Hamburglar, Grimace, Captain Crook, the Fry Guys and Ronald, to name a few. But in 1972, the chain changed their advertising focus to the adult sector. By 1975, they realized a balance was needed between the adult and child market, this was accomplished by offering breakfast to the busy businessperson and cheeseburgers, McDonaldland Cookies and hot apple pies to their families for dinner. In 1979, McDonald's introduced the ultimate in child-oriented marketing—the Happy Meal.

Impressed with the success of Burger Chef's Triple Play and *Star Wars* Funmeals, McDonald's reportedly set out to create their own kid's meal. The first Happy Meal was tested in 1978; the official start of the Happy Meal was June 1979 with the Circus Wagon Happy Meal. Their Happy Meal tie-in with *Star Trek: The Movie* may have come as a result of Burger Chef's *Star Wars* promotion. The *Star Trek* Happy Meal was enormously popular and perfectly timed. It was the beginning of an era.

McDonald's has dominated the fast food industry in general; it is only natural that they dominate the world of fast food premiums. They were able to secure the most lucrative licensing agreements and distribute the most toys. Their marketing clout made their toys the most collectible, most desirable and the most abundant ones made.

Their most successful promotion to date was the Teenie Beanie Baby Happy Meal of 1997. A second Teenie Beanie Baby promotion followed in 1998. While these promotions were the most popular, they were flawed. Caught off guard by the craziness caused by the first Teenie Beanie Happy Meal, McDonald's tried to meet the demands of collectors by setting up specific rules and regulations regarding the purchase of Happy Meals and toys during the 1998 promotion. The Beanie Baby craze was at its zenith. Any attempt made by McDonald's to control the distribution of the Teenie Beanies, while well intentioned, was futile. In order to meet the demands of Teenie Beanie Baby collectors, fast food toy collectors, and

! Remember, prices given are for individual pieces only, not complete sets.

the kids who just wanted a Happy Meal, McDonald's increased the production of the 1999 series (reportedly 350 million were made), laid out very specific rules and made sure the buying public was aware of these rules before the promotion began. It seemed the public had tired of the Teenies, or maybe the rumors of increased production numbers were true. Either way, the third promotion did not meet with the same success as the previous two.

McDonald's Happy Meal toys have continued to be the most collectible and desirable. Collector's clubs have been formed throughout the country and conventions are held annually. For more information or to join, send a self-addressed-stamped envelope to McDonald's Collector's Club, PMB 200, 1153 S. Lee St., Des Plaines, IL 60016-6503 or visit them on the World Wide Web at www.mcdclub.com.

TOY NAME / DESCRIBE	YEAR	EX	MINT
101 Dalmatians	1991	1	3
set of four: Lucky, Pongo, Sergeant Tibbs, Cruella			
101 Dalmatians	1996	3	10
101 different PVC dogs. Premiums were randomly distributed in opaque bag and were un-named. Values for each dog can vary due to the haphazzard distribution.			
101 Dalmatians Snow Globes	1996	2	5
set of four: Snowman's Best Friend (snowman), Snow Furries (dome with red ribbon), Dog Sledding (sleigh), Dalmatian Celebration (number 101)			
101 Dalmatians the Series	1997	1	2
set of eight flip cars: Perdita/Scorch, Two-Tone/Lt. Pug, Lucky/Cruella, Rolly/Ed Pig, Steven/Sydney, Tripod/Dumpling, Cadpig/Spot, Pongo/Swamprat			
3-D Happy Meal	1981	20	40
set of four cartons with 3-D designs and 3-D glasses inside: Bugsville, High Jinx, Loco Motion, Space Follies			
A Bug's Life	1998	1	2
set of eight wind-ups: Dim, Rosie, Dot, Flik, Francis, Heimlich, Hopper, Atta			
A Bug's Life Watches	1998	2	3
set of three: Leafy Ant-icks with 3-D face, Pop Topper with flip-top lid, Bug Eye Spy with two floating characters			
Adventures of Ronald McDonald	1981	6	12
set of seven rubber figures: Ronald, Birdie, Big Mac, Captain Crook, Mayor McCheese, Hamburglar, Grimace			

TOY NAME	DESCRIBE	YEAR	EX	MINT
Airport Happy Meal set of five: Birdie Bentwing Blazer, Fry Guy Flyer, Grimace Bi-Plane, Big Mac Helicopter, Ronald Sea Plane		1986	2	4
Airport Happy Meal set of two U3 toys: Fry Guy Friendly Flyer, Grimace Smiling Shuttle		1986	3	5
Aladdin and the King of Theives one U3 toy: Abu squirter		1996	1	3
Aladdin and the King of Thieves set of eight: Cassim, Abu, Jasmine, Iago, Genie, Sa'luk, Aladdin, Maitre d'Genie		1996	1	3
Alvin and The Chipmunks set of four figures: Simon with movie camera, Theodore with rap machine, Brittany with juke box, Alvin with guitar		1991	4	8

101 Dalmatians Display, McDonald's, 1991.

101 Dalmatians Flip-over Cars, McDonald's, 1997.

Other side of Dalmatian Flip-over Cars, McDonald's.

! Remember, prices given are for individual pieces only, not complete sets.

101 Dalmatians Snow Globes, McDonald's, 1996.

Front of Animaniacs Bag, McDonald's, 1994.

Astrosnicks II, McDonald's, 1984. Photo courtesy Museum of Science and Industry, Chicago.

TOY NAME	DESCRIBE	YEAR	EX	MINT
Alvin and The Chipmunks one U3 toy: Alvin leaning on jukebox		1991	10	20

Amazing Wildlife
    set of eight plush animals: Asiatic Lion,
    Chimpanzee, Koala Bear, African
    Elephant, Dromedary Camel, Galapagos
    Tortoise, Siberian Tiger, Polar Bear
		1995	1	2

An American Tail
    set of four books: Fievel and Tiger, Fievel's
    Friends, Fievel's Boat Trip, Tony and
    Fievel
		1986	2	3

Animal Kingdom
    set of thirteen: triceratops, tcucan, gorilla
    and baby, elephant, dragon, iguanodon,
    lion, cheetah, zebra, rhino, crocodile,
    ringtail lemur, tortoise (only available at
    McDonald's in Wal-Mart stores); four
    special collector's cups were available with
    super sized combo meal
		1998	1	2

Animal Pals
    set of six plush toys: Panda, Rhinoceros,
    Yak, Moose, Brown Bear, Gorilla
		1997	1	2

Animal Riddles
    set of eight rubber figures: condor, snail,
    turtle, mouse, anteater, alligator, pelican,
    dragon, in various colors
		1979	2	4

Astrosnicks III, McDonald's, 1985. Photo courtesy Museum of Science and Industry, Chicago.

! Remember, prices given are for individual pieces only, not complete sets.

TOY NAME	DESCRIBE	YEAR	EX	MINT
Animaniacs	set of eight: Bicycle Built for Trio, Goodskate Goodfeathers, Upside-Down Wakko, Slappy and Skipper's Chopper, Dot's Ice Cream Machine, Midy and Buttons Wild RideYakko Ridin' Ralph, Pink and the Brain Mobile	1994	2	3
Animaniacs	set of eight: Pinky & the Brain, Goodfeathers, Dot & Ralph, Wacko & Yakko, Slappy & Skippy, Mindy & Buttons, Wakko, Yakko & Dot, Hip Hippos	1995	1	2
Animaniacs	set of four U3 toys: Bicycle Built for Trio, Goodskate Goodfeathers, Yakko Ridin' Ralph, Mindy and Buttons Wild Ride	1995	3	5
Astrosnick Spacemobile	9-1/2" rocket ship available with four Happy Meal Cosmic Coupons	1984	30	60
Astrosnicks I	set of eight: eight different 3" rubber space creatures: Scout, Thirsty, Robo-Robot, Laser, Snickapotamus, Sport, Skater, Astralia	1983	8	30
Astrosnicks II	set of six: Copter, Drill, Ski, Racing, Perfido, Commander	1984	8	30

Babe, McDonald's, 1996.

Front of Back to the Future Bag, McDonald's, 1992.

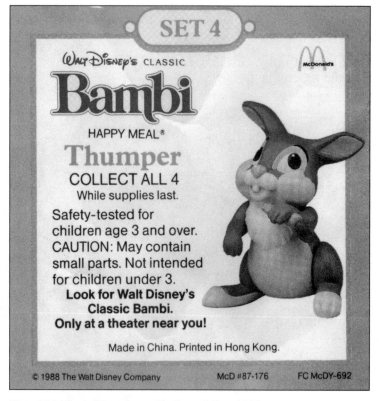

Bambi Insert, Thumper, McDonald's, 1988.

! Remember, prices given are for individual pieces only, not complete sets.

TOY NAME	DESCRIBE	YEAR	EX	MINT
Astrosnicks III	set of eleven figures: C.B., Banner, Commander, Junior, Jet, Laser, Perfido, Pyramido, Robo-Robot, Astralia, Snikapotamus; regionally distributed in the Oklahoma area, many are the same as other Astroniks but without "M" marking	1985	10	40
Attack Pack/Polly Pocket	set of four: Ruck, Battle Bird, Lunar Invader, Sea Creature; joint promotion with Polly Pocket	1995	1	2
Attack Pack/Polly Pocket	one U3 toy: Truck	1995	2	3
Babe	set of seven plush toys: Babe, Ferdinand, Fly, Maa, Cow, Mouse, Dutchess	1996	1	2
Back to the Future	set of four: Doc's DeLorean, Verne's Jukebox, Marty's Hoverboard, Einstein's Traveling Train	1992	1	2
Bambi	set of four figures: Owl, Flower, Thumper, Bambi	1988	2	4
Bambi	set of three U3 toys: Bambi with butterfly on tail, Bambi, Thumper	1988	5	10
Barbie and Friends/World of Hot Wheels	set of eleven: Bicyclin' Barbie, Jewel and Glitter Shani, Camp Barbie, Camp Teresa, Locket Surprise Ken, African-American Locket Surprise Barbie, Caucasian Locket Surprise Barbie, African-American Jewel and Glitter Barbie, Caucasian Jewel and Glitter Barbie, Bridesmaid Skipper; joint promotion with Hot Wheels	1994	2	5
Barbie/Hot Wheels	set of four Barbie figures with dioramas: Movie Star with SuperStar Barbie; In Concert with Solo in the Spotlight Barbie; Tea Party with Enchanted Evening Barbie; Moonlight Ball with 1989 Happy Holiday Barbie. Test Market Happy Meal, regionally distributed in Savanah, Georgia; joint promotion with Hot Wheels	1990	25	125

TOY NAME	DESCRIBE	YEAR	EX	MINT
Barbie/Hot Wheels set of eight: Ice Capades, All American, Lights & Lace, Hawaiian Fun, Happy Birthday, Costume Ball, Wedding Day Midge, My First Barbie		1991	2	3
Barbie/Hot Wheels set of two U3 toys: Costume Ball Barbie, Wedding Day Midge; joint promotion with Hot Wheels		1991	2	4
Barbie/Hot Wheels set of eight: My First Ballerina, Birthday Party, Western Stamping, Romantic Bride, Hollywood Hair, Paint 'n Dazzle, Twinkle Lights, Secret Hearts; joint promotion with Hot Wheels		1993	2	3

Barbie/Hot Wheels, McDonald's, 1991. Photo courtesy Museum of Science and Industry, Chicago.

Batman, the Animated Series, McDonald's, 1993. Photo courtesy Museum of Science and Industry, Chicago.

! Remember, prices given are for individual pieces only, not complete sets.

Front of Batman Bag, McDonald's, 1992.

Bedtime, McDonald's, 1989.

← 213

**Behind the Scenes,
McDonald's, 1992.**

TOY NAME	DESCRIBE	YEAR	EX	MINT
Barbie/Hot Wheels	set of ten: Hot Skatin' Barbie, Dance Moves Barbie, Butterfly Princess Teresa, Cool Country Barbie, Caucasian Lifeguard Ken, African-American Lifeguard Ken, Caucasian Lifeguard Barbie, African-American Lifeguard Barbie, Bubble Angel Barbie, Ice Skatin' Barbie; joint promotion with Hot Wheels	1995	2	3
Barbie/Hot Wheels	one U3 toy: figurine of blond girl wearing green dress	1995	2	3
Barbie/Hot Wheels	set of five: Dutch Barbie, Kenyan Barbie, Japanese Barbie, Mexican Barbie, USA Barbie; joint promotion with Hot Wheels	1996	1	3
Barbie/Hot Wheels	one U3 toy: Barbie slide puzzle	1996	2	3
Barbie/Hot Wheels	set of five: Wedding Rapunzel Barbie, Rapunzel Barbie, Angel Princess Barbie, Blossom Beauty Barbie, Happy Holidays Barbie; joint promotion with Hot Wheels	1997	1	3
Barbie/Hot Wheels	set of four: Barbie, Teen Skipper, Eating Fun Kelly, Bead Blast Christie; joint promotion with NASCAR Hot Wheels	1998	1	3
Barbie/Hot Wheels Mini-Streex	set of eight dolls: Sparkle Eyes, Roller Blade, Rappin' Rockin', My First Ballerina, Snap 'N PLay, Sun Sensation, Birthday Surprise, Rose Bride; joint promotion with Hot Wheels Mini-Streex	1992	1	2
Barbie/Hot Wheels Mini-Streex	one U3 toy: Sparkle Eyes Babie	1992	2	5
Batman	set of four: Batmobile, Batmissle, Catwoman Cat Coupe, Penguin Roto-Roadster	1992	1	2
Batman Cups	set of six cups; offered in conjunction with Happy Meal	1992	1	2
Batman, the Animated Series	set of eight: Batman with removable cape, Robin, Batgirl, Two Face, Poison Ivy, Joker, Catwoman with leopard, Riddler	1993	2	3

! Remember, prices given are for individual pieces only, not complete sets.

TOY NAME	DESCRIBE	YEAR	EX	MINT
Batman, the Animated Series	one U3 toy: Batman without removable cape	1993	2	5
Beach Ball	set of three inflatables: Ronald waving, red; Birdie with sandcastle, blue; Grimace with beach umbrella, yellow. Regionally distributed in Washington, New York and Colorado	1986	10	15
Beach Ball Characters	set of three: Grimace in kayak, Ronald holding flag and beachball, Birdie in sailboat	1985	5	8
Beach Toy II	set of eight: Ronald and Grimace sand pail with yellow lid and shovel, Birdie Seaside Submarine, Fry Kid Super Sailor, Fry Kids Sand Castle Pail, Grimace Beach Ball, Birdie Shovel, Ronald Squirt Gun Rake, Ronald Fun Flyer	1990	2	3
Beach Toys I	set of four: Birdie Seaside Submarine, Grimace Bouncin' Beachball, Fry Kid Super Sailor, Ronald Fun Flyer; test market Happy Meal	1989	10	15
Beachcomber Happy Meal	set of three sand pails with shovels: Grimace, Mayor McCheese, Ronald	1986	5	10
Bedtime	set of four: Ronald toothbrush with tube of Crest toothpaste, Ronald bath mitt, Ronald Nite Stand Star Figure, Ronald cup	1989	3	6
BeetleBorgs Metallix	set of six: Stinger Drill, Beetle Bonder, Hunter Claw, Platinum Purple BeetleBorg Covert Compact, Chromuim Gold BeetleBorg Covert Compact, Titanium Silver BeetleBorg Covert Compact	1997	1	2
Behind the Scenes	set of four: Cartoon Wheel, Rainbow Viewer, Rub 'N' Draw, Balance Builder	1992	2	3
Berenstain Bears I	set of four figures: Papa with wheelbarrow, Mama with shopping cart, Brother with scooter, Sister with sled; test market set, distributed in Evansville, Indiana	1986	30	75

TOY NAME	DESCRIBE	YEAR	EX	MINT
Berenstain Bears II	set of four figures with flocked heads: Papa with wheelbarrow, Mama with shopping cart, Brother with scooter, Sister with wagon	1987	2	4
Berenstain Bears II	set of two U3 toys with paper punch outs: Mama, Papa	1987	5	10
Berenstain Bears Story Books	set of eight books: Attic Treasure Story Book, Attic Treasure Activity Book, Substitute Teacher Story Book, Substitute Activity Book, Eager Beavers Story Book, Eager Beavers Activity Book, Life with Papa Story Book, Life with Papa Activity Book	1990	2	4
Bicycle Reflector Stickers	set of four: Big Mac, Captain Cook, Hamburglar, Ronald McDonald; part of round-top Happy Meal test	1978	6	12
Bigfoot	set of eight Ford trucks: Bronco, green or orange; Pickup purple or orange; Ms. Pickup, turquoise or pink; Shuttle, red or black; each had McDonald's "M" logo on back window	1987	3	5

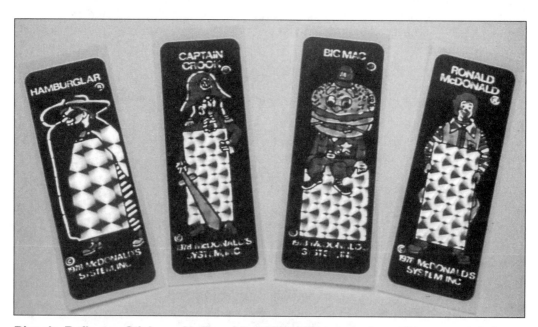

Bicycle Reflector Stickers, McDonald's, 1978. Photo courtesy Museum of Science and Industry, Chicago.

! Remember, prices given are for individual pieces only, not complete sets.

Birthday Book, McDonald's, 1983. Photo courtesy Museum of Science and Industry, Chicago.

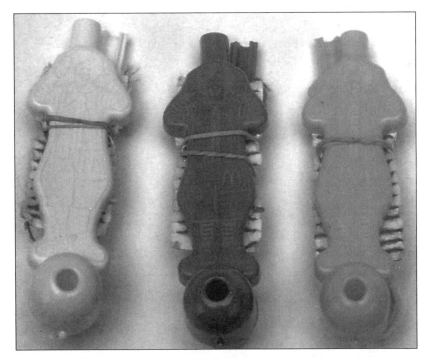

Blow String Whistle, McDonald's, 1981. Photo courtesy Museum of Science and Industry, Chicago.

TOY NAME	DESCRIBE	YEAR	EX	MINT
Bigfoot	set of eight Ford trucks: Bronco, green or orange; Pickup, purple or orange; Ms. Pickup, turquoise or pink; Shuttle, red or black; without McDonald's "M" logo on back window	1987	5	10
Birdie Bike Horn	Japanese		4	9
Birdie Magic Trick	green or orange		2	5
Birthday Book	unpunched	1983	10	15
Black History	two coloring books: Little Martin Jr. Coloring Book Volume One, Little Martin Jr. Coloring Book Volume Two; sold in six Detroit stores	1988	200	500
Blow String Whistle	set of two: red and white, yellow and white	1981	10	15
Boats 'n Floats	set of four vaccuform boats with stickers: Chicken McNugget lifeboat, Birdie float, Fry Guys raft, Grimace ski boat	1987	5	10
Bobby's World	set of four: Wagon-Race Car, Innertube-Submarine, Three Wheeler-Space Ship, Skates-Roller Coaster	1994	1	2
Bobby's World	one U3 toy: Bobby in intertube	1994	1	3
Breakfast Happy Meal	squeeze bottle with Minute Maid logo	1991	1	3
Cabbage Patch	one U3 toy: Anne Louise "Ribbons & Bows"	1992	1	2
Cabbage Patch Kids/Tonka	set of five: Tiny Dancer, Holiday Pageant, Holiday Dreamer, Fun On Ice, All Dressed Up; joint promotion with Tonka	1992	2	3
Cabbage Patch Kids/Tonka	set of four: Mimi Kristina, Abigail Lynn, Kimberly Katherine, Michelle Elyse; joint promotion with Tonka	1994	1	3

! Remember, prices given are for individual pieces only, not complete sets.

TOY NAME	DESCRIBE	YEAR	EX	MINT
Cabbage Patch Kids/Tonka	one U3 toy: SaraJane; joint promotion with Tonka	1994	2	3
Camp McDonaldland	set of four: Grimace Canteen, Birdie Mess Kit, Fry Kid Utensils, Ronald Collapsible Cup (also U3 premium)	1990	2	3
Captain Crook Bike Reflector	blue plastic, Canada	1988	1	3
Captain Crook Hat	cardboard hat that was given away with the purchase of Fish Sanwhich and fries	1976	15	20

Bobby's World, McDonald's, 1994.

Bobby's World, McDonald's, 1994.

Front of Bobby's World Bag, McDonald's, 1994.

Camp McDonaldland, McDonald's, 1990.

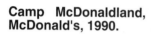

Front of Camp McDonaldland Bag, McDonald's, 1990.

! Remember, prices given are for individual pieces only, not complete sets.

TOY NAME	DESCRIBE	YEAR	EX	MINT
Castlemaker	set of four vacuuform molds: dome, square, cylinder, rectangle; regionally distributed in Michigan and Houston, Texas	1987	20	40
Changeables	set of six figures that change into robots, with painted hands: Big Mac, Milk Shake, Egg McMuffin, Quarter Pounder, French Fries, Chicken McNuggets	1987	4	8
Chip 'N Dale's Rescue Rangers	set of four figures: Chip's Whirly-Cuptor, Dale's Roto-Roadster, Gadgets Rescue Racer, Monteray Jack's Propel-A-Phone	1989	2	4
Chip 'N Dale's Rescue Rangers	set of two U3 toys: Gadget's Rockin', Chip's Rockin Racer	1989	2	5
Christmas Ornaments	Fry Guy and Fry Girl, cloth, 3-1/2" tall	1987	3	6
Christmas Stocking	plastic, "Merry Christmas to My Pal"	1981	3	6
Circus	set of nine: Fun House Mirror with Ronald, Fun House Mirror with Hamburglar, Acrobatic Ronald, French Fry Faller, Strong Gong with Grimace, Punchout Midway: The Ronald Midway, Punchout Midaway: Fun House, Punchout Tent with Grimace, Punchout Tent with Birdie	1983	15	25
Circus Parade	set of four: Ringmaster Ronald McDonald, Bareback Rider Birdie, Grimace Playing Caliope, Elephant Trainer Fry Guy	1991	2	4

Captain Crook Hat, McDonald's, 1976. Photo courtesy Museum of Science and Industry, Chicago.

Changeables, McDonald's, 1987.

Changeables, McDonald's, 1987.

! Remember, prices given are for individual pieces only, not complete sets.

TOY NAME	DESCRIBE	YEAR	EX	MINT
Circus Wagon		1979	2	3
	set of four rubber toys: poodle, chimp, clown, horse			
Colorforms Happy Meal		1986	10	15
	set of five: Beach set, Grimace; Farm set, Ronald; Camping set, Professor; Play set, Birdie; Picnic, Hamburglar			
Colorforms Happy Meal		1986	10	20
	two U3 sticker sets: Beach set, Grimace; Farm set, Ronald			

Chip 'N Dale's Rescue Rangers Insert, Gadget's Rescue Racer, McDonald's, 1989.

Chip 'N Dale's Rescue Rangers Insert, Chip's Whirly-Cupter, McDonald's, 1989.

Chip 'N Dale's Rescue Rangers Insert, U3 toy: Gadget's Rockin' Rider, McDonald's, 1989.

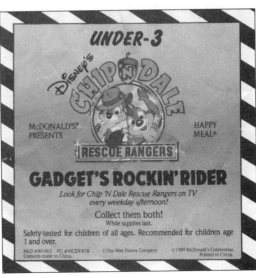

TOY NAME	DESCRIBE	YEAR	EX	MINT
Colorful Puzzles-Japan	set of three: Dumbo, Mickey & Minnie, Dumbo & Train		5	10
Coloring Stand-Ups	characters and backgrounds to color, punch out and stand	1978	4	8
Combs	set of four: Captain Crook, red; Grimace, yellow; Ronald, yellow, blue or purple; Grimace Groomer, green	1988	1	2
Commandrons	set of four robots: Solardyn, Magna, Motron, Velocitor	1985	5	15
Connectables	set of four: Birdie on tricycle, Grimace in wagon, Hamburglar in airplane, Ronald in soapbox racer	1991	3	5
Construx	set of four: axle, wing, body cylinder, canopy; spaceship could be built from all four premiums	1986	10	25
CosMc Crayola	set of five coloring kits: four crayons with coloring page, thin red marker with coloring page, four chalk with chalkboard, washable thin marker with coloring page, three paints and brush with paint-by-number page	1988	5	10
CosMc Crayola	one U3 toy: two fluorescent crayons with coloring page	1988	5	10
Crayola Happy Meal	set of five kits: triangle stencil with green marker, rectangular stencil with four fluorescent crayons, triangle stencil with orange marker, traingle stencil with thin blue marker, triangle stencil with thin red marker	1986	10	15
Crayola II	set of four stencils: Grimace with four fluorescent crayons, Hamburglar with four crayons, Birdie with thick orange or green marker, Ronald with thin blue or red marker	1987	2	5

! Remember, prices given are for individual pieces only, not complete sets.

Colorforms Happy Meal, McDonald's, 1986. Photo courtesy Museum of Science and Industry, Chicago.

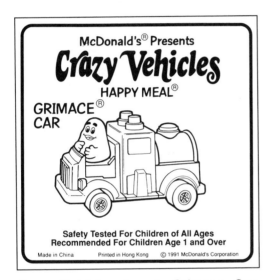

Crazy Vehicles Insert, Grimace Car, McDonald's, 1991.

Crazy Vehicles Insert, Hamburglar Train, McDonald's, 1991.

Crazy Vehicles Insert, Ronald McDonald Buggy, McDonald's, 1991.

TOY NAME	DESCRIBE	YEAR	EX	MINT
Crayola II	one U3 stencil: Ronald on fire engine with four crayons	1987	5	10
Crayola Squeeze Bottle, Kay Bee	set of four: regional promotion		3	6
Crayon Squeeze Bottle	set of four: blue, green, yellow, red; regionally distributed in New York state and Connecticut	1992	3	5
Crazy Creatures with Popoids	set of four made up of two bellows and one connector: red and blue bellows with wheel joint; yellow and blue connectors with ball joint; yellow and red bellows with cube joint; red and yellow with seven-sided joint	1985	6	12
Crazy Vehicles	set of four: Ronald in red car, Hamburglar in yellow train engine, Grimace in green car, Birdie in pink airplane	1991	3	5
Design-O-Saurs	set of four: Ronald on Tyrannosaurus, Grimace on Pterodactyl, Fry Guy on Brontosaurus, Hamburglar on Triceratops	1987	5	10
Dexterity Games	set of two: "McDonald's," "McDonald's Look for the Golden Arches starts fresh ... every day"; regionally distributed in Columbus, Ohio	1965	75	100
Dink the Little Dinosaur	set of six figures with diorama and description: Dink, Flapper, Amber, Crusty, Scat, Shyler	1990	4	12
Dino-Motion Dinosaurs	set of six: Baby, Grandma, Robbie, Earl, Fran, Charlene	1993	1	2
Dino-Motion Dinosaurs	one U3 toy: Baby squirter	1993	2	4
Dinosaur Days	set of six rubber dinos: Pteranodon, Triceratops, Stegosaurus, Dimetrodon, T-Rex, Ankylosaurus	1981	1	2
Dinosaur Talking Storybook	set of four books and tape: The Dinosaur Baby Boom, Danger Under the Lake, The Creature in the Cave, The Amazing Birthday Adventure	1989	5	10

! Remember, prices given are for individual pieces only, not complete sets.

TOY NAME	DESCRIBE	YEAR	EX	MINT
Discover the Rain Forest	set of four activity books with punch out figures: Sticker Safari, Wonders in the Wild, Paint It Wild, Ronald and the Jewel of the Amazon Kingdom	1991	2	4
Disney Favorites	set of four activity books: Lady and the Tramp, Dumbo, Cinderella, The Sword in the Stone	1987	3	4
Disney Masterpiece Collection	figures in video-shaped box	1996	1	2
Disney Video Favorites	set of six: The Spirit of Mickey, Lady & the Tramp, Pocahontas: Journey to a New World, Mary Poppins, The Black Cauldron, Flubber	1998	1	2

Dexterity Games, McDonald's, 1965. Photo courtesy Museum of Science and Industry, Chicago.

Dino-Motion Dinosaurs Display, McDonald's, 1993.

Dino-Motion Dinosaurs, McDonald's, 1993.

Disney Video Favorites, McDonald's, 1998.

! Remember, prices given are for individual pieces only, not complete sets.

TOY NAME	DESCRIBE	YEAR	EX	MINT
Disneyland 40th Anniversary Viewers	set of nine: Brer Brer on Space Mountain; Aladdin & Jasmine at Aladdin's Castle; Roger Rabbit in Mickey's Toontown; Winnie the Pooh on Big Thunder Mountain with viewer, green cab; Winnie the Pooh on Big Thunder Mountain with viewer, black cab; Simba in The Lion King Celebration; Mickey Mouse on Space Mountain; Peter Pan in Fantasmic!; King Louie on the Jungle Cruise	1995	1	2
Disneyland 40th Anniversary Viewers	one U3 toy: Winnie the Pooh on Big Thunder Mountain without viewer (green cab)	1995	2	3
Double Bell Alarm Clock	wind-up alarm clock with silver bells, hammer ringer, silver feet, image of Ronald on face with head tilted over folded hands, as if asleep		20	40
Duck Tales I	set of four toys: Telescope, Duck Code Quacker, Magnifying Glass, Wrist Decoder	1988	2	4
Duck Tales I	one U3 toy: Motion Magic Map	1988	2	5
Duck Tales II	set of four toys: Uncle Scrooge in red car; Launchpad in plane; Huey, Dewey and Louie on jet ski; Webby on blue trike	1988	3	6
Duck Tales II	one U3 toy: Huey on skates	1988	15	20
Dukes of Hazzard	set of six white plastic cups: Luke, Boss Hogg, Bo, Sheriff Roscoe, Daisy, Uncle Jesse	1982	3	6
Dukes of Hazzard	set of five vaccuform container vehicles, Boss Hogg's Caddy, Daisy's Jeep, Sheriff Roscoe's Police Car, Uncle Jesse's Pickup, General Lee; each container came with sticker sheet; regionally distributed in Missouri	1982	20	50
E.T.	set of four posters: E.T. with boy and girl in front of spaceship, E.T. with boy and bike, E.T. with glowing finger, E.T. with radio	1985	8	12

TOY NAME	DESCRIBE	YEAR	EX	MINT
Earth Days	set of four: birdfeeder, globe terrarium, binoculars, tool carrier with shovel	1994	1	2
Earth Days	one U3 toy: tool carrier with shovel	1994	1	2
Earth Days	one U3 toy: tool carrier with shovel	1994	1	2
Eric Carle Finger Puppets	set of six puppets: The Very Quiet Crickett, The Very Lonely Firefly, A House for Hermit Crab, The Grouchy Ladybug, The Very Hungry Caterpillar, The Very Busy Spider	1996	1	2
Fast Macs I	set of four pull-back action cars: Big Mac in white police car, Ronald in yellow Jeep, Hamburglar in red racer, Birdie in pink convertible	1984	3	5

Duck Tales II Insert, Huey, Dewey & Louie on Surf Ski, McDonald's, 1988.

Duck Tales II Insert, Launchpad in plane, McDonald's, 1988.

! Remember, prices given are for individual pieces only, not complete sets.

Fast Macs I, McDonald's, 1984.

Fast Macs II, McDonald's, 1985.

Fisher-Price U3 Toys, McDonald's, 1997.

TOY NAME	DESCRIBE	YEAR	EX	MINT
Fast Macs II	set of four pull-back action cars: Big Mac in white police car, Ronald in yellow Jeep, Hamburglar in red racer, Birdie in pink convertible	1985	3	5
Favorite Friends	set of seven character punch-out cards	1978	2	5
Feeling Good	set of six grooming toys: Grimace soap dish, Fry Guy sponge, Birdie mirror, Ronald toothbrush, Hamburglar toothbrush, Captain Crook comb	1985	1	3
Feeling Good	set of two U3 floating toys: Grimace in Tub, Fry Guys on Duck	1985	5	8
Field Trip	set of four: Kaleidoscope, Leaf Printer, Nature Viewer, Explorer Bag	1993	1	2
Field Trip	one U3 toy: Nature Viewer	1993	1	2
Fisher-Price U3 Toys	set of 24: Balls in ball, Barn Puzzle, Bear in Train, Birdie in Poppity-Pop Car, Bus, Clock, Corn Popper, Cow Book, Dog Squeek, Dog Roll-A-Rounds, Dog in House, Dog on Red Wheels, Grimace Roll-A-Rounds, Horse, Jeep, Key Ring, Man in Poppity-Pop Car, Truck, Fun Sounds Ball, Puzzle Maze, Ronald McDonald in Drive-thru, Pig in Barrel, Radio Rattle, Chatter Telephone. In 1996, McDonald's began offering generic Fisher-Price toys as the U3 premium for Happy Meals.	1996	2	4
Fisher-Price U3 Toys	set of 24: McDonald's child size drink, McDonald's small french fries, McDonald's apple pie, McDonald's Chicken McNuggets, Grimace and Ronald at McDonald's, Little People Dalmatian in a Fire Truck, Little People Pilot and Airplane, Little People Ronald in Boat, Little People Hamburgler in hanburger car, Little People Farmer in Tractor, cellular phone, radio, ring toss, Little People green roll ball, camera, large and small elephant, blue dog, stacking blocks	1997	2	4

! Remember, prices given are for individual pieces only, not complete sets.

TOY NAME	DESCRIBE	YEAR	EX	MINT
Flintstone Kids	set of four figures in animal vehicles: Betty, Barney, Fred, Wilma	1988	4	8
Flintstone Kids	one U3 toy: Dino figure	1988	10	20
Flintstones	set of five: Fred at Bedrock Bowl-O-Rama, Betty and Bamm Bamm at Roc Donald's, Wilma at the Flinstone's house, Barney at the Fossil Fill-Up, Pebbles and Dino at Toy-S-Aurus	1994	1	2
Flintstones	one U3 toy: Rocking Dino	1994	3	5
Florida Beach Ball	set of three with Florida logo: Grimace in kayak, Ronald holding flag and beachball, Birdie in sailboat	1985	20	25

Flintstones Insert, Barney & Fossil Fill-up, McDonald's, 1994.

Flintstones Insert, Wilma & the Flintstone's House, McDonald's, 1994.

Food Fundamentals: Ruby the Apple and Otis the Sandwich with arms extended, McDonald's, 1993.

Food Fundamentals: Ruby the Apple and Otis the Sandwich, McDonald's, 1993.

Fraggle Rock II, McDonald's, 1988.

! Remember, prices given are for individual pieces only, not complete sets.

TOY NAME	DESCRIBE	YEAR	EX	MINT
Food Fundamentals	set of four: Slugger the steak; Otis the sandwhich, Milly the milk carton, Ruby the apple	1993	1	2
Food Fundamentals	one U3 toy: Dunkan the ear of corn	1993	1	2
Fraggle Rock I	set of four: Gobo Fraggle, Bulldoozer and Friends, Cotterpin Doozer and Friends, Cotterpin Doozer; test market Happy Meal, regionally distributed in West Virginia	1987	20	40

Fraggle Rock Insert, Boober & Wembly Fraggle, McDonald's, 1988.

Fraggle Rock Insert, Red Fraggle, McDonald's, 1988.

Fry Benders, McDonald's, 1990.

TOY NAME	DESCRIBE	YEAR	EX	MINT
Fraggle Rock II	set of four: Gobo in carrot car, Red in radish car, Mokey in eggplant car, Wembly and Boober in pickle car	1988	1	2
Fraggle Rock II	set of two U3 toys: Gobo holding carrot, Red holding radish	1988	4	6
French Fry Radio	large red fry container with fries	1977	12	25
Friendly Skies	set of two: Ronald in white plane, Grimace in white plane	1991	5	10
Friends of Barbie/World of Hot Wheels	one U3 toy: Barbie Ball; joint promotion with Hotw Wheels	1994	2	3
Fry Benders	set of four figures: Grand Slam with baseball glove, Froggy with scuba tanks, Roadie with bicycle, Freestyle with rollerskates	1990	5	10
Fry Guy Cookie Cutter	Fry Guy on unicycle, green or orange	1987	1	3
Fun Ruler	white platic ruler featuring Mayor McCheese, Fry Guys, Birdie, Ronald, Grimace, Hamburglar	1983	3	5
Fun To Go	set of seven cartons with games and activities	1977	2	4
Fun with Food	set of four: Hamburger Guy, Fry Guy, Soft Drink Guy, Chicken McNugget Guys	1989	3	6
Funny Fry Friends	set of eight: Too Tall, Tracker, Rollin' Rocker, Sweet Cuddles, Zzz's, Gadzooks, Matey, Hoops	1990	2	4
Funny Fry Friends	two U3 toys: Lil' Chief, Little Darling	1990	3	5
Funny Fry Guys	set of four: Gadzooks, Matey, Zzz's, Tracker; test market Happy Meal, regionally distributed in California, Pennsylvania, Maryland	1989	15	25

! Remember, prices given are for individual pieces only, not complete sets.

Fun with Food Insert, Hamburger Guy, McDonald's, 1989.

Fun with Food Insert, French Fry Guy, McDonald's, 1989.

Fun with Food Insert, Soft Drink Guy, McDonald's, 1989.

Fun with Food, Chicken McNuggets Guy, McDonald's, 1989.

TOY NAME	DESCRIBE	YEAR	EX	MINT
Furby	eight different designs done in ten different color combinations; there are a total of 80 diffferent Furby toys available. Each toy comes packaged in opage bags so the collector doesn't know which Furby they have	1999	5	10
Garfield	set of four: Garfield on skateboard, Garfield on tricycle, Garfield in car, Garfield on scooter; test market Happy Meal; regionally distributed in Erie, Pennsylvania and Charlston, South Carolina	1988	20	50
Garfield II	set of two U3 toys: Garfield Skating, Garfield with Pooky	1989	2	5
Garfield II	set of four: Garfield on Scooter, Garfield on Skateboard, Garfield in Jeep, Garfield with Odie on Motorscooter	1989	3	6

Funny Fry Friends Insert, Gadzooks, McDonald's, 1989.

! Remember, prices given are for individual pieces only, not complete sets.

Funny Fry Friends Insert,
Hoops, McDonald's.

Funny Fry Friends Insert,
Matey, McDonald's.

Funny Fry Friends Insert,
Rollin' Rocker, McDonald's.

TOY NAME	DESCRIBE	YEAR	EX	MINT
Glo-Tron Spaceship	set of four vacuform spaceships: red, blue, green, gray; each spaceship came with set of glow-in-the-dark stickers	1986	25	50
Glow in the Dark Yo-Yo	no markings or dates	1978	2	5
Going Places/Hot Wheels	set of fourteen: Corvette Stingray, Jeep CJ-7, 3-Window '34, Baja Breaker, Chevy Citation, Firebird Funny Car, Land Lord, Malibu Grand Prix, 380-SEL, Minitrek, P-928, Sheriff Patrol, Split Window '63, Turismo	1983	12	20
Golf Ball	marked with McDonald's logo		1	3
Good Morning	set of four: Ronald toothbrush, McDonaldland comb, Ronald clock, white plastic cup	1991	1	2

Funny Fry Friends Insert, Sweet Cuddles, McDonald's.

! Remember, prices given are for individual pieces only, not complete sets.

Funny Fry Friends Insert,
Too Tall, McDonald's.

Funny Fry Friends Insert,
Tracker, McDonald's.

Funny Fry Friends Insert, U3
toy: Lil' Chef, McDonald's.

TOY NAME	DESCRIBE	YEAR	EX	MINT
Good Sports		1984	8	12
	set of six puffy stickers: Hamburglar, Mayor McCheese, Ronald, Sam the Olympic Eagle, Birdie, Grimace			
Good Times Great Taste Record			2	4
Gravedale High		1991	2	3
	set of four mechanical Halloween figures: Cleofatra, Frankentyke, Vinnie Stoker, Sid the Invisible Kid			
Gravedale High		1991	3	5
	one U3 toy: Cleofatra			
Grimace Bank		1985	10	20
	purple ceramic, 9" tall			
Grimace Pin			6	12
	enamel			

Funny Fry Friends Insert, U3 toy: Little Darling, McDonald's.

Funny Fry Friends Insert, Zzz's, McDonald's.

! Remember, prices given are for individual pieces only, not complete sets.

Gravedale High, McDonald's, 1991.

Halloween, McDonald's, 1995.

Hook, McDonald's, 1991.

TOY NAME	DESCRIBE	YEAR	EX	MINT
Grimace Ring		1970	8	15
Grimace Sponge			2	4
	Grimace, Grimace Car Wash			
Halloween		1995	1	2
	set of four cassete tapes: Ronald Makes it Magic, Travel Tunes, Silly Sing-Along, Scary Sound Affects			

Front of Hook Bag, McDonald's, 1991.

Hot Wheels/Barbie, McDonald's, 1993.

! Remember, prices given are for individual pieces only, not complete sets.

TOY NAME	DESCRIBE	YEAR	EX	MINT
Halloween	set of four figures: Hamburglar with witch costume, Grimace with ghost costume, Ronald with Frankenstein soctume, Birdie with pumpkin costume	1995	2	3
Halloween	one U3 toy: pumpkin with pop-up Grimace	1995	2	3
Halloween Buckets	set of three pumpkin-shaped pails: McGoblin, McPumpkin, McBoo	1986	2	4
Halloween Buckets	set of three pumpkin-shaped pails: McBoo, McGoblin, McPunk'n	1987	2	3
Halloween Buckets	set of three: Ghost, Witch, Pumpkin	1989	1	3
Halloween Buckets	set of three pumpkin-shaped pails: orange pumpkin, white glow-in-dark ghost, green witch	1990	2	4
Halloween Buckets	set of three pumpkin-shaped pails with cut-out lids: Ghost, Witch, Pumpkin	1992	1	2
Halloween Buckets	set of three with cookie-cutter lids: Ghost, Whitch, Pumpkin	1994	1	3
Halloween Happy Meal	set of five pumpkin-shaped pails: McGoblin, McPunk'n, McPunky, McBoo, McBoo; regionally distributed in the northeast, marked with 1985 copyright	1985	12	15
Halloween McNugget Buddies	set of six: Pumpkin McNugget, McBoo McNugget, Monster McNugget, McNuggula McNugget, Witchie McNugget, Mummie McNugget	1993	1	3
Halloween McNugget Buddies	one U3 toy: McBoo McNugget	1993	3	5
Halloween McNugget Buddies	set of six: Dragon, Spider, Fairy Princess, Alien Monster, Rock Star, Ronald	1996	2	3
Halloween Pumpkin Ring	orange pumpkin face		1	3
Hamburglar Doll	7" stuffed doll by Remco; one of set of seven, sold on blister card	1976	12	25

TOY NAME	DESCRIBE	YEAR	EX	MINT
Hamburglar Hockey		1979	2	4
Happy Holidays	set of two cards with stickers: Gingerbread House, Train	1984	15	20
Happy Meal From the Heart	set of two scratch-and-sniff Valentines: Grimace: Valentine You Shake Me Up!; Ronald: Valentine You Warm My Heart!	1990	2	3
Happy Pail	set of three: pink pail with purple shovel, shows Ronald and Mayor McCheese under umbrella with purple shovel; white pail with yellow shovel, shows Ronald in intertube; white pail with slotted yellow shovel, shows airplane pulling banner; distributed in the New York state and New England area only	1983	25	35
Happy Pail III	set of five sand pails with either yellow shovel or red rake: Beach with blue lid, Parade with orange lid, Treasure Hunt with red lid, Vacation with green lid, Picnic with yellow lid	1986	5	10
Happy Pails, Olympics	set of four with shovels: Swimming, blue; Cycling, yellow; Athletics, beige; Olympic Games, white	1984	1	3
Happy Teeth	set of two: Reach toothbrush, tube of toothpaste	1983	15	20
Hat Happy Meal	set of four: Birdie green derby, Fry Guy orange safari hat, Grimace yellow construction hat, Ronald red fireman hat	1990	10	15
Hercules	set of ten: Wind Titan & Hermes, Rock Titan & Zeus, Hydra & Hercules, Lava Titan & Baby Pegasus, Cyclops & Pain, Fates & Panic, Pegasus & Megara, Ice Tita & Calliope, Nessus & Phil, Cerberus & Hades	1997	1	2
Hercules Plates	set of six: Hercules, Megara, Pegasus, Zeus, Muses, Phil; over-the-counter premium offered for $1.99 with food purchase and $2.99 without purchase	1997	3	5

! Remember, prices given are for individual pieces only, not complete sets.

Hot Wheels/Barbie, McDonald's, 1996.

Hot Wheels/Barbie, McDonald's, 1997.

Front of Jungle Book Bag, McDonald's, 1990.

Little Mermaid Bag, McDonald's, 1989.

TOY NAME	DESCRIBE	YEAR	EX	MINT
Hercules Sports Toys	set of eight: Zeus football, Hades stopwatch, Hercules sport bottle, Eye of Fates foot bag, Pain and Panic sound stick, Hercules medal, Phil megaphone, Whistling Discus	1998	1	2
High Flying Kite Happy Meal	set of three kites: Hamburglar, Birdie, Ronald; regionally distributed in New England area	1986	200	225

Furby, Mc Donald's 1999.

M-Squad: Spynocular (closed), McDonald's, 1993.

M-Squad: Spynocular (open), McDonald's, 1993.

! Remember, prices given are for individual pieces only, not complete sets.

TOY NAME	DESCRIBE	YEAR	EX	MINT
Hobby Box		1985	10	15
	set of four plastic boxes: yellow, green, red, blue; regionally distributed in the Southern United States			
Honey, I Shrunk the Kids Cups		1988	1	2
	set of three white 20 oz. plastic cups: Giant Bee, On the Dog's Nose, Riding the Ant			
Hook		1991	1	2
	set of four: Peter Pan, Mermaid, Rufio, Hook			
Hot Wheels Mini-Streex/Barbie		1992	2	3
	one U3 toy: Orange Arrow car; joint promotion with Barbie			
Hot Wheels Mini-Streex/Barbie		1992	2	4
	set of eight: Flame-Out, Quick Flash, Turbo Flyer, Black Arrow, Hot Shock, Racer Tracer, Night Shadow, Blade Burner; joint promotion with Barbie			
Hot Wheels/Barbie		1988	10	15
	set of twelve: Streat Beast, silver or red; P-911, white or black; Split Window '63, silver or black; '57 T-Bird, turquoise or white; 80's Firebird, blue or black; Sheriff Patrol; Fire Patrol			
Hot Wheels/Barbie		1990	50	100
	set of four: Corvette, white; Ferrari, red; Hot Bird, silver; Camaro, turquoise; test market Happy Meal, regionally distributed in Savanah, Georgia; joint promotion with Barbie			
Hot Wheels/Barbie		1991	2	3
	set of eight cars: '55 Chevy, white or yellow; '63 Corvette, green or black; Camaro Z-28, purple or orange; '57 T-Bird, turquoise or red; joint promotion with Barbie			
Hot Wheels/Barbie		1991	2	3
	one U3 tool set: yellow wrench and red hammer; joint promotion with Barbie			
Hot Wheels/Barbie		1993	2	3
	set of eight: Quaker State Racer #62, McDonald's Dragster, McDonald's Thunderbird #27, Hot Wheels Dragster, McDonald's Funny Car, Hot Wheels Funny Car, Hot Wheels Camaro #1, Duracell Racer #88; joint promotion with Barbie			

TOY NAME	DESCRIBE	YEAR	EX	MINT
Hot Wheels/Barbie	one U3 tool set: blue wrench and yellow hammer; joint promotion with Barbie	1993	2	3
Hot Wheels/Barbie	set of eight: Lightning Speed, Shock Force, Blue Bandit, Power Circuit, Twin Engine, Radar Racer, Back Burner, After Blast; joint promotion with Barbie	1995	2	3
Hot Wheels/Barbie	one U3 toy: Key Force car; joint promotion with Barbie	1995	2	3
Hot Wheels/Barbie	set of five: Flame Series, Roarin' Road Series, Dark Rider Series, Hot Hubs Series, Krakel Car Series; joint promotion with Barbie	1996	1	2
Hot Wheels/Barbie	one U3 toy: Hot Wheels squeek toy; joint promotion with Barbie	1996	1	3
Hot Wheels/Barbie	set of five: Tow Truck, Taxi, Police Car, Ambulance, Fire Truck; joint promotion with Barbie	1997	1	2
Hunchback of Notre Dame	set of eight: Esmeralda Amulet, Scepter, Clopin Mask, Hugo Horn, Clopin Puppet Drum, Juggling Balls, Tambourine, Quasimodo Bird Catcher	1997	1	2
I Like Bikes	set of four bike accessories: Ronald Basket, Grimace mirror, Birdie spinner, Fry Guy Horn	1990	10	20
Jungle Book	set of four wind-up figures: Baloo the bear, Shere Kahn the tiger, King Louie the orangutan, Kaa the snake	1990	1	3
Jungle Book	set of two U3 toys: Junior, Mowgli	1990	3	6
Jungle Book	set of six: Baloo, Junior, Bagheera, King Louie, Kaa, Mowgli	1997	1	2
Kissyfur	set of eight figures: four non-flocked figures—Floyd, Gus, Kissyfur, Jolene; the flocked and non-flocked fiugres make up one complete set	1987	5	10

! Remember, prices given are for individual pieces only, not complete sets.

TOY NAME	DESCRIBE	YEAR	EX	MINT
Kissyfur	four flocked figures—Beehonie, Duane, Toot, Lennie	1987	15	40
Lego Building Set III	four different sets: tanker boat, blue; airplane, green; roadster, red; helicopter, yellow	1986	3	5
Lego Building Sets	set of four Duplo U3 toys: blue blocks, Bird, red blocks, green Duplo blocks	1983	5	10
Lego Building Sets	set of four: ship, helicopter, truck, airplane	1983	25	40
Lego Building Sets II	set of four: ship, truck, helicopter, airplane	1984	3	5
Lego Building Sets II	set of two U3 toys: Duplo bird, Duplo boat with sailor	1984	4	8
Lego Building Sets III	set of two U3 toys: Duplo bird, Duplo boat	1986	3	5
Lego Motion IV	set of two U3 Duplo toys: Giddy the Gator, Tuttle the Turtle	1989	2	5
Lego Motion IV	set of eight kits: Gyro Bird, Lightning Striker, Land Laser, Sea Eagle, Wind Whirler, Sea Skimmer, Turbo Force, Swamp Stinger	1989	3	6
Linkables	set of four: Birdie on tricycle, Ronald in soap-box racer, Grimace in wagon, Hamburglar in airplane; regionally distributed in New England area	1993	2	4
Lion Circus	set of four rubber figures: bear, elephant, hippo, lion	1979	2	3
Little Engineer	set of four floting toys: Grimace Happy Taxi, green or yellow; Birdie, green or yellow	1987	2	6
Little Engineer	set of five vacuform train engines: Birdie Sunshine Special, Fry Girl's Express, Fry Guy's Flyer, Grimace Streak, Ronald Railway	1987	4	8

TOY NAME	DESCRIBE	YEAR	EX	MINT
Little Gardener	set of four: Ronald Water Can, Birdie Shovel with Marigold seeds, Grimace Rake with radish seeds, Fry Guy Planter	1989	1	2
Little Gardener	one U3 toy: Birdie shovel	1989	1	3
Little Golden Books	set of five books: Country Mouse and City Mouse, Tom & Jerry, Pokey Little Puppy, Benji, Monster at the End of This Block	1982	2	4
Little Mermaid	set of four: Flounder, Ursula, Prince Eric, Ariel with Sebastian	1989	1	3
Little Mermaid	set of eight: Ursula, Flounder, Scuttle, Ariel, Max, Glut, Eric, Sebastian	1997	1	2
Little Mermaid, Gold	set of eight: Ursula, Flounder, Scuttle, Ariel, Max, Glut, Eric, Sebastian; one out of every ten toys distributed with Happy Meal was a gold toy; compete sets of gold Little Mermaid premiums could be ordered for $12.99 plus shipping with forms available at McDonald's	1997	4	7
Little Travelers with Lego Building Sets	set of four: airplane, boat, helicopter, car; regionally distributed in Oklahoma; similar to Lego Building Set Happy Meal	1985	20	30
Littlest Pet Shop/Transformers Beast Wars	set of four: Swan, Unicorn, Dragon, Tiger; joint promotion with Transformers Beast Wars	1996	1	2
Littlest Pet Shop/Transformers Beast Wars	one U3 toy: Hamster Wheel; joint promotion with Transformers Beast Wars	1996	1	2
Looney Tunes Christmas Dolls-Canada	set of four: Sylvester in nightgown and cap, Tasmanian Devil in Santa hat, Bugs in winter scarf , Tweetie dressed as Elf		3	6
Looney Tunes Quack Up Cars	set of five: Taz Tornado Tracker, Porky Ghost Catcher, Bugs Super Stretch Limo in red or orange, Daffy Splittin' Sportster	1993	3	5

! Remember, prices given are for individual pieces only, not complete sets.

Mac Tonight Insert, Mac Tonight in Jeep, McDonald's, 1988.

Mac Tonight Insert, Mac Tonight on motorcycle, McDonald's, 1988.

Mac Tonight Insert, Mac Tonight in Airplane, McDonald's, 1988.

Mac Tonight, McDonald's, 1988.

TOY NAME	DESCRIBE	YEAR	EX	MINT
Looney Tunes Quack Up Cars	one U3 toy: Bugs Bunny Swingin' Sedan in red or orange	1993	3	5
Luggage Tags	set of four: Birdie, Hamburglar, Grimace, Ronald	1988	3	5
Lunch Box	set of four lunch boxes: Grimace at bat, Ronald playing football, Ronald on rainbow, Ronald flying spaceship	1987	5	10
M-Squad	set of four: Spystamper, Spytracker, Spynocular, Spycoder	1993	1	2
M-Squad	one U3 toy: Spytracker watch	1993	1	2
Mac Tonight	set of six: Mac in Jeep, Mac in sports car, Mac on Surf Ski (with or without wheels), Mac on Motorcycle (red or black), Mac in Airplane (wearing blue or black sun-glasses), Mac on Scooter; given out from 1988 to 1990, Surf Ski with wheels and Airplane with dark sunglasses were distributed in 1990	1988	4	8

Mac Tonight Insert, U3 toy: Mac Tonight on Skateboard, McDonald's, 1988.

Mac Tonight Insert, Mac Tonight on Scooter, McDonald's, 1988.

! Remember, prices given are for individual pieces only, not complete sets.

Front of Marvel Super Heroes, Human Torch, McDonald's, 1996.

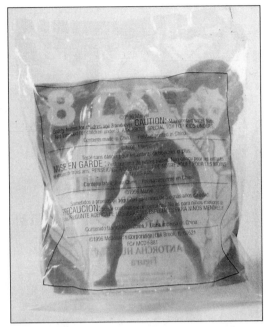

Back of Marvel Super Heroes packaging, Human Torch, McDonald's, 1996.

McDino Changeables, McDonald's, 1991.

McDino Changeables, McDonald's, 1991.

TOY NAME	DESCRIBE	YEAR	EX	MINT
Mac Tonight Pin Moonface and slogan enamel pin		1988	2	4
Mac Tonight Puppet Fingertronic foam puppet		1988	6	15
Mac Tonight Sunglasses adult size		1988	2	5
Magic School Bus set of four: Collector Card Kit, Space Tracer, Geo Fossil Finder, Undersea Adventure Game with yellow tab		1994	1	2
Magic School Bus one U3 toy: Undersea Adventure Game without yellow tab		1994	1	2
Magic Show set of five tricks: String Trick, Disappearing Hamburger Patch, Magic Tablet, Magic Picture—Ronald, Magic Picture—Grimace		1985	3	6
Makin' Movies set of four: Sound Effects Machine, Movie Camera, Clapboard with chalk, Megaphone		1994	1	2
Makin' Movies one U3 toy: Sound Effects Machine		1994	1	2
Marvel Super Heroes set of eight: Spider-Man, Storm, Wolverine, Jubilee, Color Change Invisible Woman, Thing, Hulk, Human Torch		1996	1	2
Marvel Super Heroes one U3 Toy: Spider-Man ball		1996	1	2
Matchbox Mini-Flexies set of eight rubber cars: Cosmobile, Hairy Hustler, Planet Scout, Hi-Tailer, Datsun, Beach Hopper, Baja Buggy		1979	2	4
McBoo Bags set of six: three McBoo bags — Witch, Ghost, Monster; three pails — McBoo, McGoblin, Witch		1991	1	2
McBunny Easter Pails set of three: Pinky, Fluffy, Whiskers		1989	3	6
McCharacters on Bikes set of four: Ronald on red tricycle, Grimace on blue tricycle, Hamburglar on yellow tricycle, Birdie on pink tricycle		1991	3	5

! Remember, prices given are for individual pieces only, not complete sets.

TOY NAME	DESCRIBE	YEAR	EX	MINT
McDino Changeables set of eight: Happy Meal-o-don, Quarter Pounder Chees-o-saur, Big Mac-o-saurus Rex, McNugget-o-saurus, Hotcakes-o-dactyl, Large Fry-o-saur, Tri-shak-atops, McDino cone		1991	2	3
McDino Changeables set of three U3 toys: Bronto Cheeseburger, Small Fry Ceratops with yellow arches, Small Fry Ceratops with red arches		1991	2	3
McDonald Sun Glasses set of four: Grimace, Birdie, Ronald, Hamburglar; over-the-counter premium offered with food purchae for 99 cents		1989	5	7
McDonald's All-Star Race Team (MAXX) '91 complete set of cards		1991	4	8
McDonald's All-Star Race Team (MAXX) '92 complete set of 36 cards		1992	4	8
McDonald's Playing Cards two decks to a set			2	5
McDonald's Spinner Top-Holland			2	4
McDonaldland Band set of eight music toys: Grimace saxophone, Fry Guy trumpet, Fry Guy boat whistle, Ronald harmonica, Ronald train whistle, Ronald pan pipes, Birdie kazoo, Hamburglar whistle		1987	1	3
McDonaldland Carnival set of four: Birdie on swing, Grimace in turn-around, Hamburglar on ferris wheel, Ronald on carousel		1990	3	5
McDonaldland Carnival one U3 floaty toy: Grimace		1990	10	15
McDonaldland Dough set of eight, each included can of modeling clay and mold: red with Ronald star mold, yellow with Ronald square mold, green with Fry Girl octagon mold, blue with Fry Guy hexagon mold, purple with Grimace square mold, orange with Grimace triangle mold, pink with Birdie heart mold, white with Birdie circle mold; sold in the Southern United States only		1990	3	5

TOY NAME	DESCRIBE	YEAR	EX	MINT
McDonaldland Express	set of four train car containers: Ronald engine, caboose, freight car, coach car	1982	15	40
McDonaldland Junction	set of four snap-together train cars: red Ronald Engine, yellow Birdie Parlor car, green Hamburger Flat Car, purple Grimace caboose	1983	5	10
McDonaldland Junction	set of four regionally distributed cars: blue Ronald Engine, pink Birdie Parlor Car, white Hambuger Flat Car, orange Grimace Caboose	1983	20	30
McDonaldland Play-Doh	set of eight colors: white, orange, yellow, purple, pink, red, green, blue	1986	2	4
McDonaldland TV Lunch Box	set of four lunch boxes: blue, green, yellow, red; each box came with a sheet of stickers; regionally distributed in New England area	1987	5	10
McDrive Thru Crew	set of four: fries in potato roadster, shake in milk carton, McNugget in egg roadster, hamburger in ketchup bottle; regionally distributed in Ohio and Illinois	1990	20	40

McDrive Thru Crew, McDonald's, 1990. Photo courtesy Museum of Science and Industry, Chicago.

! Remember, prices given are for individual pieces only, not complete sets.

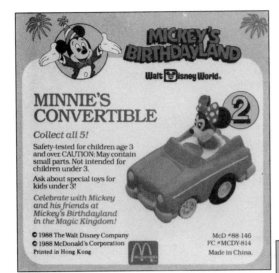

Mickey's Birthdayland Insert, Minnie's Convertible, McDonald's, 1989.

Mickey's Birthdayland Insert, Goofy's Sport-Coupe, McDonald's, 1989.

Mighty Duck the Animated Series, McDonald's, 1997.

TOY NAME	DESCRIBE	YEAR	EX	MINT
McNugget Buddies	set of ten rubber figures and accessories: Sparky, Volley, Corny, Drummer, Cowpoke, Sarge, Snorkel, First Class, Rocker, Boomerang	1989	1	2
McNugget Buddies	set of two U3 toy: Slugger, Daisy	1989	1	2
Metrozoo Happy Meal	set of four: Elephant, Chimp, Flamingo, Tiger; distributed only in South Florida	1987	25	75
Michael Jordan Fitness Fun Challenge	set of eight: baseball, basketball, flying disc, football, jump rope, soccer ball, squeeze bottle, stop watch; all premiums are marked with Michael Jordan logo	1992	2	4
Mickey and Friends Epcot Center '94 Adventure	set of eight: Donald in Mexico, Daisy in Germany, Mickey in U.S.A., Minnie in Japan, Chip in China, Pluto in France, Dale in Moroco, Goofy in Norway	1994	2	3

Mighty Mini 4x4s Insert, Dune Buster, McDonald's, 1991.

! Remember, prices given are for individual pieces only, not complete sets.

Mix 'Em Up Monsters Insert,
Corkle, McDonald's.

Mix 'Em Up Monsters Insert,
Gropple, McDonald's.

Mix 'Em Up Monsters Insert,
Thugger, McDonald's.

TOY NAME	DESCRIBE	YEAR	EX	MINT
Mickey and Friends Epcot Center '94 Adventure one U3 toy: Mickey in U.S.A.		1994	2	3

Mickey's Birthdayland
    set of five characters in vehicles: Minnie's
    Convertible, Donald's Train, Goofy's
    Jalopy, Mickey's Roadster, Pluto's
    Rumbler
		1989	3	5

Mickey's Birthdayland
    set of four U3 vehicles: Mickey's
    Convertible, Goofy's Car, Minnie's
    Convertible, Donald's Jeep
		1989	5	10

Micro Machines/Sky Dancers
    set of four: Evac Copter, Polar Explorer,
    Ocean Flyer, Deep Sea Hunter; joint
    promotion with Sky Dancers
		1997	1	2

Mighty Duck the Animated Series
    set of four: Wildwing, Nosedive, Mallory,
    Duke L'Orange
		1997	1	2

Mighty Mini 4x4s
    set of four: Cargo Climber, Dune Buster,
    L'il Classic, Pocket Pickup
		1991	1	2

Mighty Mini 4x4s one U3 toy: Pocket Pickup		1991	3	5

Mighty Morphin Power Rangers
    set of four: Power Com, Powermorpher
    Buckle, Alien Detector, Power Siren
		1995	1	2

Mighty Morphin Power Rangers one U3 toy: Power Flute		1995	1	2

Minnesota Twins Baseball Glove
    Twins logo on side, Coca-Cola inside glove,
    McDonald's satin logo on back, given to the
    first 100 kids at 1984 Twins game
		1984	40	75

Mix 'em Up Monsters
    set of four: Thuggle, Blibble, Corkle,
    Gropple; regionally distributed in St. Louis,
    Missouri and Northern California
		1989	2	5

Moveables
    set of six vinyl bendies: Birdie, Captain
    Crook, Fry Girl, Hamburglar, Professor,
    Ronald; regionally distributed in St Louis,
    Missouri area
		1988	5	15

! Remember, prices given are for individual pieces only, not complete sets.

TOY NAME	DESCRIBE	YEAR	EX	MINT
Mulan	set of eight: Mulan, Kahn, Little Brother, Shan-Yu, Mushi, Shang-Li, Cri-Kee, Chien-Po, Ling, Yao	1998	1	2
Muppet Babies holiday promotion	set of four stuffed toys: Miss Piggy, Kermit, Fozzie; over-the-counter premium sold with food purchase for for $1.99	1988	2	5
Muppet Babies I	set of four: Kermit with skateboard, Miss Piggy with car and flat hair ribbon, Gonzo with tricycle and no shoes, Fozzie with horse; test market Happy Meal, regionally distributed in Savannah, Georgia	1986	25	50
Muppet Babies II	set of four: Kermit with skateboard, Miss Piggy with pink car, Gonzo with tricycle and shoes, Fozzie with horse	1987	2	4
Muppet Babies II	set of two U3 toys: Kermit on skates, Miss Piggy on Skates	1987	3	5

Back of Mystery of the Lost Arches Insert, McDonald's.

Mystery of the Lost Arches Insert, Magic Lens Camera, McDonald's.

Mystery of the Lost Arches Insert, Flashlight/Telescope, McDonald's.

Mystery of the Lost Arches Insert, Phone/Periscope, McDonald's.

Mystery of the Lost Arches Insert, Micro-Cassette/Magnifier, McDonald's.

! Remember, prices given are for individual pieces only, not complete sets.

TOY NAME	DESCRIBE	YEAR	EX	MINT
Muppet Babies III	set of four: Miss Piggy on tricycle, Gonzo in airplane, Fozzie in wagon, Kermit on soapbox racer	1991	2	4
Muppet Kids	set of four: Kermit with red tricycle, Miss Piggy with pink tricycle, Gonzo with yellow tricycle, Fozzie with green tricycle	1989	25	50
Muppet Treasure Island	one U3 toy: Bath Book "The Muppet Treasure Island"	1996	1	2
Muppet Treasure Island	set of four: Miss Piggy, Kermit, Gonzo, Fozzy Bear	1996	2	3
Muppet Workshop	set of four: Bird, Dog, What-Not, Monster	1995	1	2
Muppet Workshop	one U3 toy: What-Not	1995	1	2
Music Happy Meal	set of four 33-1/3-rpm records: If You're Happy/Little Bunny Foo Foo; Do the Hokey Pokey/Eensy Weensy Spider; Boom, Boom, Ain't it Great to Be Crazy; She'll be Comin' 'Round the Mountain, Head, Shoulders, Knees and Toes	1985	3	5
My Little Pony/Transformers	set of six: Minty, Snuzzle, Blossom, Cotton Candy, Blue Belle, Butterscotch; joint promotion with Transformers; regionally distributed in St. Louis, Missouri area	1985	20	60
My Little Pony/Transformers	set of three: Ivy, Sundance, Light Heart; split promotion with Transformers	1998	1	2

New Archies, McDonald's, 1988. Photo courtesy Museum of Science and Industry, Chicago.

TOY NAME	DESCRIBE	YEAR	EX	MINT
Mystery Happy Meal set of five: Detective Kit, Crystal Ball, Ronald Magni-Finder, Birdie Mangi-Finder, Fry Guys Magni-Finder		1983	20	35
Mystery of the Lost Arches set of five: Phone/Periscope, Flashlight/Telescope in red and blue or red and yellow, Magic Lens Camera, Microcaste/Magnifier		1992	1	2
Mystic Knights of Tir na Nog set of eight: Rohan, Queen Maeve, Angus. Tore, Deirdre, mider, Ivar, Lugad; a bonus toy can be built from Queen Maeve, Tore, Mider and Lugad		1999	1	3
NASCAR Hot Wheels/Barbie set of four: Ronald Happy Meal NASCAR, Mac Tonight, Hot Wheels, 50th Anniversary NASCAR; split promotion with Barbie;		1998	1	3
Nature's Helpers set of five: Double Digger with cucumber seeds, Bird Feeder, Watering Can, Terrarium with coleus seeds, Rake with marigold seeds		1991	1	2
Nature's Watch set of four: Bird Feeder, Double Shovel-Rake, Greenhouse, Sprinkler		1992	1	2
Nature's Watch one U3 toy: double shovel-rake		1992	1	2
New Archies set of six figures in bumper cars: Moose, Reggie, Archie, Veronica, Betty, Jughead; regionally distributed in St. Louis, Missouri area		1988	5	15
New Food Changeables set of eight with painted hands: Krypto Cup, Fry Bot, Turbo Cone, Macro Mac, Gallacta Burger, Robo Cakes, C2 Cheeseburger, Fry Force		1989	2	4
Nickelodeon set of four: Blimp Game, Loud-Mouth Mike, Gotcha Gusher, Applause Paws		1993	1	2

! Remember, prices given are for individual pieces only, not complete sets.

New Food Changeables Insert, C2
Cheeseburger, McDonald's, 1989.

New Food Changeables Insert,
Fry Bot, McDonald's, 1989.

New Food Changeables Insert,
Fry Force, McDonald's, 1989.

TOY NAME	DESCRIBE	YEAR	EX	MINT
Nickelodeon		1993	1	2
	one U3 toy: Blimp squirter			
Nickelodeon's Tangle Toy		1997	1	2
	set of eight Twist-a-zoids			
Norman Rockwell Brass Ornament		1983	3	7
	50th Annivesary Norman Rockwell design, gift packaged with McDonald and Coca-Cola logos			
Norman Rockwell Ornament		1978	3	7
	clear acrylic, "Christmas Trio," gift boxed			

New Food Changeables Insert, Gallacta Burger, McDonald's, 1989.

New Food Changeables Insert, Macro Mac, McDonald's, 1989.

! Remember, prices given are for individual pieces only, not complete sets.

New Food Changeables with one U3 toy, McDonald's, 1989.

Oliver & Company Insert, Dodger, McDonald's, 1988.

Oliver & Company Insert, Francis, McDonald's, 1988.

TOY NAME	DESCRIBE	YEAR	EX	MINT
Old McDonald's Farm	set of six figures: farmer, wife, rooster, pig, sheep, cow; regionally distributed in Missouri and Tennessee	1986	3	12
Old West	set of six rubber figures: cowboy, frontiers-man, lady, Indian, Indian woman, sheriff	1981	7	14
Oliver & Company	set of four finger puppets: Oliver, Georgette, Francis, Dodger	1988	3	5

Oliver & Company, McDonald's, 1988.

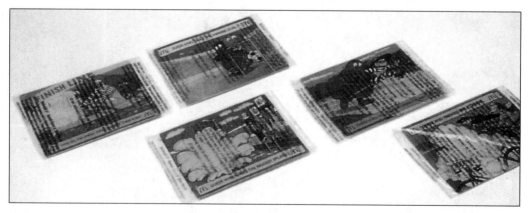

Olympic Sports, McDonald's, 1984. Photo courtesy Museum of Science and Industry, Chicago.

❗ Remember, prices given are for individual pieces only, not complete sets.

2|4

Peanuts, McDonald's, 1990. Photo courtesy Museum of Science and Industry, Chicago.

Front of Peanuts Bag, Lucy's Apple Cart, McDonald's, 1990.

Front of Peanuts Bag, Snoopy's Hay Hauler, McDonald's, 1990.

TOY NAME	DESCRIBE	YEAR	EX	MINT
Olympic Beach Ball	set of three: Grimace in kayak, green; Ronald holding flag and beachball, red; Birdie in sailboat, blue	1984	15	20
Olympic Sports	set of five Guess'n'Glow puzzles: Guess Which Guy Comes in Under the Wire (Grimace and Hamburglar), Guess Who Makes the Biggest Splash (Ronald, Birdie and Captain); Guess Who Finished Smiles Ahead (Hamburglar and Birdie); Who Do You Know That Can Help them Row? (Ronald and Fry Guy); Guess Who Stole the Winning Goal (Grimace); this promotion replaced the original Olympics Sports Happy Meal	1984	15	30
Olympic Sports	set of five zip-action toys: Ronald on bicycle, roller skating Birdie, Grimace, Birdie and Captain rowing, running Grimace; prototypes only. The Olympic sports Happy Meal was cancelled after the toys failed safety tests. It was replaced by Guess'n'Glow puzzles	1984	15	30
Olympic Sports II	set of six clip-on buttons: Birdie/gymnastics, Hamburglar/track and field, CosMc/basketball, Fry Girl/diving, Ronald/bicycling, Grimace/soccer	1988	5	10
On the Go I	set of five: On the Go Bead Game, Stop & Go Bead Game, Ronald Magic Slate, Hamburglar Magic Slate, On the Go Transfers	1985	10	15
On the Go Lunch Box II	set of four: red lunch box with bulliten board and stickers, green lunch box with bulliten board and stickers, yellow lunch bag with Ronald, white lunch bag with Grimace	1988	2	4
Out of Fun Happy Meal	set of four: Balloon Ball, Ronald Bubble Shoe Wand, Sunglasses, Sand Pail	1993	1	2
Paint with Water	paintless coloring board with self contained frame and easel	1978	5	10

! Remember, prices given are for individual pieces only, not complete sets.

TOY NAME	DESCRIBE	YEAR	EX	MINT
Peanuts	set of four: Snoopy's Hay Hauler, Charlie Brown's Seed Bag 'N Tiller, Lucy's Apple Cart, Linus' Milk Mover	1990	2	4
Peanuts	set of two U3 toys: Charlie Brown's egg basket or Snoopy's potato sack	1990	3	6
Peanuts, Canadian	set of four: Snoopy as Red Baron, Woodstock in race car, Charlie Brown in blue train, Lucy in fire truck	1989	3	6
Pencil Puppets	six different pencil toppers in shapes of McDonaldland characters	1978	2	4
Peter Pan	set of seven: Peter Pan Glider, Tic Tock Croc, Captain Hook Spyglass, Tinker Bell Lantern Clip, Smee Light, Wendy & Michael Magnifier, Activity Tool	1998	1	2
Peter Rabbit	set of four books: The Tale of Benjamin Bunny, The Tale of Peter Rabbit, The Tale of the Flopsy Bunnies, The Tale of Squirrel Nutkin; regionally distributed in Pennsylvania and New York	1988	10	25
Picture Perfect	set of four Crayola products: coloring (thin) marker, red or blue; drawing (thick) marker, orange or green; box of three fluorescent Cayons; box of six Crayons	1985	5	10
Piggsburg Pigs	set of four: Rembrandt, Huff & Puff, Piggy & Crackers, Portly & Pighead; regionally distributed in Florida, Colorado and Ohio	1991	3	5
Play-Doh	set of four containers of Play-Doh: blue, red, yellow, white; regionally distributed in the New England area; containers did not have any McDonald's markings	1983	15	20
Play-Doh II	set of two containers of Play-Doh: pink and green	1985	5	10
Play-Doh III	set of eight containers of Play-Doh: pink, blue, purple, green, red, yellow, white, orange	1986	5	8

TOY NAME	DESCRIBE	YEAR	EX	MINT
Playmobile	set of five toys and accesories: farmer, sheriff, Indian, umbrella girl, horse and saddle	1982	10	20
Polly Pocket/Attack Pack	set of four: Ring, Locket, Watch, Bracelet; joint promotion with Attack Pack	1995	1	2
Polly Pocket/Attack Pack	one U3 toy: watch	1995	2	3

Raggedy Ann and Andy Insert, Grouchy Bear with a carousel, McDonald's, 1992.

Raggedy Ann and Andy Insert, Raggedy Andy with a slide, McDonald's, 1989.

! Remember, prices given are for individual pieces only, not complete sets.

Raggedy Ann and Andy Insert, Raggedy Ann with a swing, McDonald's, 1989.

Raggedy Ann and Andy Insert, The Camel with the Wrinkled Knees with a seesaw, McDonald's, 1989.

Raggedy Ann and Andy Insert, U3 toy: The Camel with the Wrinkled Knees, McDonald's, 1989.

TOY NAME	DESCRIBE	YEAR	EX	MINT
Popoids	set of six made up of two to three bellows and one joint piece: blue and dark blue bellows with one ball joint; blue and white bellows with cube joint; blue and dark blue bellows with one cube joint; red and yellow bellows with pentahedron joint; red and yellow bellows with wheel joint; blue, dark blue and yellow bellows without joint; regionally distributed in the St. Louis, Missouri area	1984	20	40
Potato Head Kids I	set of twelve: Lumpy, Potato Dumpling, Big Chip, Smarty Pants, Dimples, Spike, Potato Puff, Tulip, Spud, Lolly, Slugger, Slick; regionally distributed in Texas, Oklahoma and New Mexico	1987	5	25

Real Ghostbusters Insert, Slimer Squeezer, McDonald's, 1992.

! Remember, prices given are for individual pieces only, not complete sets.

Rescuers Down Under,
McDonald's, 1990.

Front of Rescuers Down Under Bag,
Cody, McDonald's, 1990.

Front of Rescuers Down Under
Bag, U3 toy: Bernard,
McDonald's, 1990.

TOY NAME	DESCRIBE	YEAR	EX	MINT
Potato Head Kids II set of eight: Dimples, Spike, Potato Dumpling, Slugger, Slick, Tulip, Potato Puff, Spud		1992	3	6
Punkin' Makins character cutouts to decorate pumpkins: Ronald, Goblin, Grimace		1977	7	15
Raggedy Ann and Andy set of four: Raggedy Andy with slide, Raggedy Ann with swing, Grouchy Bear merry-go-round, Camel with Wrinkled Knees with teeter totter		1989	5	10
Raggedy Ann and Andy one U3 toy: Camel with Wrinkled Knees		1989	8	12
Read Along with Ronald set of four books and tapes: Grimace Goes to School, The Day Birdie the Early Bird Learned to Fly, The Mystery of the Missing French Fries, Dinosaur in McDonaldland		1989	5	10
Real Ghostbusters set of five school tools: pencil case, notepad, ruler, pencil with pencil topper, pencil sharpener		1987	3	5
Real Ghostbusters set of four: Ecto Siren, Egon Spinner, Slimer horn, water bottle; regionally distributed in Kansas City, Kansas		1992	3	5
Real Ghostbusters one U3 toy: Slimer squirter		1992	5	10
Recess set of seven: TJ, Spinelli, Vince, Mikey, Gretchen, Gus, School Teacher		1998	1	2
Records set of four 45-rpm records in sleeves with different songs and colored labels		1985	3	6
Rescuers Down Under set of four slide-viewing movie camera toys: Jake, Wilbur, Bernard and Bianca, Cody		1990	2	4
Rescuers Down Under One U3 toy: Bernard		1990	3	6
Rescuers Down Under Christmas Ornament set of two: Miss Bianca, Bernard		1990	3	6

! Remember, prices given are for individual pieces only, not complete sets.

TOY NAME	DESCRIBE	YEAR	EX	MINT
Rings	set of five rings with character heads: Big Mac, Captain Crook, Grimace, Hamburglar, Ronald	1977	5	10
Roger Rabbit Scarf-Japan	McDonald's logo, Japanese writing on scarf	1988	10	20
Ronald and Pals Haunted Halloween	set of six: Birdie, Gramace, Iam Hungry, Hamburglar, Ronald, McNugget Buddy	1998	1	2
Ronald McDonald Celebrates Happy Birthday	set of sixteen: Ronald McDonald, Barbie, Hot Wheels, E.T., Sonic the Hedgehog, Berenstain Bears, Tonka, Cabbage Patch Kids, 101 Dalmatians, Little Mermaid, Muppet Babies with white tie, Muppet Babies with blue tie, Peanuts, The Little Mermaid, Tiny Toons, Happy Meal Guys	1994	3	5
Ronald McDonald Celebrates Happy Birthday	one U3 toy: Ronald McDonald	1994	3	5
Ronald McDonald Cookie Cutter	Ronald with balloons, green or orange	1987	1	3
Ronald McDonald Doll	14" vinyl head with a soft body by Dakin		15	35
Ronald McDonald Doll	7" doll by Remco		18	25
Ronald McDonald Maze	lift up mystery game	1979	4	10
Ronald McDonald Pin	enamel, Ronald in Christmas wreath		6	12
Ronald McDonald Plastic Flyers	Ronald with legs and arms extended, red or yellow		1	3
Ronald McDonald Shoe & Sock Game-Japan	plastic with ball and string, with Japanese writing		5	10
Ronald McDonald Tote Bag-Japan	writing in Japanese		5	10
Runaway Robots	set of six: Skull, Jab, Flame, Beak, bolt, Coil; regionally distributed in Nebraska, Maine, Massachusettes, Tenessee and Alabama	1987	4	10

TOY NAME	DESCRIBE	YEAR	EX	MINT
Safari Adventure		1980	2	4
	six different rubber animals: alligator, monkey, gorilla, tiger, hippo, rhinoceros			
Sailors		1988	4	8
	set of two U3 floating toys: Grimace in speedboat, Fry Guy on intertube			
Sailors		1988	5	10
	set of four floating toys: Hamburglar Sailboat, Ronald Airboat, Grimace Submarine, Fry Kids Ferry			

Sonic 3 The Hedgehog, McDonald's, 1994. Photo courtesy Museum of Science and Industry, Chicago.

Sky-Busters, McDonald's, 1982.

! Remember, prices given are for individual pieces only, not complete sets.

**Space Raiders,
McDonald's 1979**

Stomper Mini 4x4, McDonald's, 1986.

Space Rescue: Tele-Communicator (closed), McDonald's, 1995.

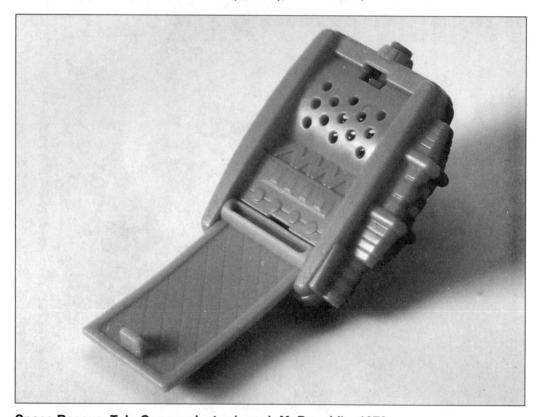

Space Rescue: Tele-Communicator (open), McDonald's, 1979.

! Remember, prices given are for individual pieces only, not complete sets.

TOY NAME	DESCRIBE	YEAR	EX	MINT
Santa Claus: The Movie	set of four books: The Elves at the Top of the World, Sleighful of Surprises, Workshop of Surprises	1985	1	3
School Days	set of twelve: Ronald pencil, Grimace pencil, Hamburglar Pencil, Ronald eraser, Grimace eraser, Hamburglar eraser, Captain Crook eraser, Birdie eraser, Grimace pencil sharpener, Ronald pencil sharpener, Ronald and Birdie ruler, Ronald and Birdie pencil case	1984	5	10
Sea World of Ohio	set of three figures: Dolly Dolphin, Penny Penguin, Shamu the whale; regionally distributed in Clevland, Ohio area	1988	8	20
Sea World of Texas	set of four stuffed toys: dolphin, penguin, walrus, whale; regionally distributed in San Antonio, Texas area	1988	5	15
Sea World of Texas II	set of five: sea otter stuffed toy, dolphin stuffed toy, whale stuffed toy, penguin sunglasses, whale sunglasses	1989	5	15
Serving Trays	set of six white plastic wedge-shaped trays: Ronald, Big Mac, Mayor McCheese, Hamburglar, Grimace, Captain Crook		3	7
Ship Shape I	set of four vacuform boat containers with stickers: Tubby Tugger, Splash Dasher, Rub-a-Dub Sub, Riverboat	1983	10	15
Ship Shape II	set of two U3 floating toys: Grimace in Tub, Fry Guys on Duck	1985	5	8
Ship Shape II	set of four vacuform boat containers with stickers: Tubby Tugger, Splash Dasher, Rub-a-Dub Sub, Riverboat; similar to 1983 Ship Shape Happy Meal but with redesigned stickers	1985	10	20
Sindy Doll	dressed in older McDonald's uniform	1970	4	8

TOY NAME	DESCRIBE	YEAR	EX	MINT
Sky Dancers/Micro Machines		1997	1	2
	set of four dancing dolls: Rosemerry, Swan Shimmer, Princess Pegasus, Flutter Fly; split promotion with Micro Machines			
Sky-Busters		1982	3	5
	set of six rubber airplanes: Skyhawk AAF, Phantom, Mirage F1, United DC-10, MIG-21, Tornado			
Sleeping Beauty		1997	1	2
	set of six: Sleeping Beauty, Maleficent, Prince Philip, Flora, Dragon, Raven			
Smart Duck		1979	2	3
	set of six rubber figures: duck, cat, donkey, chipmunk, two rabbits			
Snow White and the Seven Dwarfs		1993	2	4
	set of nine: Snow White with wishing well, Prince on horse with green base, Prince on horse without base, Queen/Witch, Bashful, Dopey and Sneezy, Doc, Happy and Grumpy, Sleepy			
Snow White and the Seven Dwarfs		1993	2	4
	one U3 toy: Dopey and Sleepy			
Sonic 3 The Hedgehog		1994	2	4
	set of four: Sonic the Hedgehog, Miles "Tails" Power, Knuckles & Dr. Ivo Robotnik			
Sonic 3 The Hedgehog		1994	3	6
	one U3 toy: Sonic Ball			
Space Aliens		1979	2	4
	set of eight rubber monsters: Lizard Man, Vampire Bat, Gill Face, Tree Monster, Winged Fish, Cyclops, Veined Brain, Insectman			
Space Jam		1996	2	4
	set of eight interlocking pieces: Lola Bunny, Bugs Bunny, Taz, Marvin the Martian, Daffy Duck, Monstar, Sylvester & Tweety, Nerdlucks			
Space Jam Plush		1996	3	5
	set of six: Lola Bunny, Bugs Bunny, Taz, Daffy Duck, Monstar, Nerdlucks			
Space Raiders		1979	2	3
	set of eight rubber aliens: Drak, Dard, flying saucer, Rocket Kryoo-5, Horta, Zama, Rocket Ceti-3, Rocket Altair-2			

! Remember, prices given are for individual pieces only, not complete sets.

TOY NAME	DESCRIBE	YEAR	EX	MINT
Space Rescue	set of four: Astro Viewer, Tele-Communicator, Space Slate, Lunar Graber	1995	1	2
Space Rescue	one U3 toy: Astro-Viewer	1995	1	2

Super Looney Tunes, McDonald's, 1991.

Super Mario Brothers Display, McDonald's, 1990.

Super Mario Brothers Insert, Koopa Paratroopa, McDonald's, 1990.

Super Mario Brothers Insert, Little Goomba, McDonald's, 1990.

! Remember, prices given are for individual pieces only, not complete sets.

TOY NAME	DESCRIBE	YEAR	EX	MINT
Spider-Man		1995	1	3
	set of eight: The Amazing Spider-Man, Dr. Octopus with moving tentacles, Mary Jane Watson with clip-on costumes, Spider-Sense Peter Parker, Scorpion Stingstriker, Spider-Man Webrunner, Venom Transport, Hobgoblin Landglider			
Spider-Man		1995	3	5
	one U3 toy: The Amazing Spider-man			
Spinner Baseball Game		1983	2	4
	green plastic with four characters			
Spinner Bicycle Game		1984	2	5
	pink or green game with two bicyclists			

Super Mario Brothers Insert, Luigi, McDonald's, 1990.

Super Mario Brothers Insert, Mario, McDonald's, 1990.

Front of Tale Spin Bag, McDonald's, 1990.

Tamagotchi Key Chains, McDonald's, 1998.

❗ Remember, prices given are for individual pieces only, not complete sets.

TOY NAME	DESCRIBE	YEAR	EX	MINT
Sports Ball	set of gour: white baseball, brown football, orange basketball, red and yellow soccer ball; regionally distributed in Kansas City and Indiana	1991	2	5
Sports Balls	set of four: basketball, baseball, football and tennis ball; test market Happy Meal, regionally distributed in Springfield, Missouri	1988	20	40
Sports Balls	one U3 toy: hard plastic baseball	1988	20	40
Sports Balls	set of four: baseball, football, basketball, soccer	1990	2	4
Star Trek	Starfleet game	1979	10	15
Star Trek	set of four glitter iron-ons: Kirk, Spock, McCoy, Ilia; packaged in pairs	1979	10	20
Star Trek	navigation bracelet with decals	1979	10	25
Star Trek	rings: Kirk, Spock, Starfleet insignia, Enterprise	1979	15	20
Star Trek	set of five video viewers, each with different story	1979	15	30
Sticker Club	set of five different sticker sheets: shiny, scratch and sniff, action stickers, puffy stickers, paper	1985	5	10
Stomper Mini 4x4	set of six: Chevy S-10 Pick-Up, blue; Chevy S-10 Pick-up, white; Chevy Van; Dodge Rampage, white; Dodge Rampage, blue; Jeep Renegade	1985	5	10
Stomper Mini 4x4	set of six push toys: Jeep Renegade, Dodge Rampage, white; Dodge Rampage, blue; Chevy S-10 Pick-up, blue; Chevy S-10 Pick-up, yellow; Chevy Van	1985	5	10

TOY NAME	DESCRIBE	YEAR	EX	MINT
Stomper Mini 4x4		1986	5	10
	set of sixteen: Toyota Tercel, blue or gray; AMC Eagle, black or orange; Chevy S-10 pickup, black or yellow; Chevy van, red or yellow; Chevy Blazer, yellow or red; Ford Ranger, orange or red; Jeep Renegade, maroon or orange; Dodge Rampage, blue or white			
Story of Texas		1986	75	100
	set of eight books: Austin series—The Beginning, Independence, The Frontier, The 20th Century; Houston series—The Beginning, Independence, The Frontier, The 20th Century; regionally distributed in Texas			
Storybook Muppet Babies		1988	2	5
	set of three books: Baby Piggy, the Living Doll; The Legend of Gimmee Gulch; Just Kermit and Me!			
Super Looney Tunes		1991	2	4
	set of four figures with costumes: Super Bugs, Bat Duck, Taz Flash, Wonder Pig			
Super Looney Tunes		1991	2	4
	one U3 toy: Bat Duck in rocking boat			
Super Mario Brothers		1990	2	4
	set of four action figures: Mario, Luigi, Little Goomba, Koopa			
Super Mario Brothers		1990	2	4
	one U3 toy: Super Mario			
Super Sticker Squares		1987	1	3
	nine scenes and over 100 reusable stickers			
Super Summer		1987	20	30
	set of three: sailboat, watering can, beachball; test market Happy Meal, distributed in Fresno, California			
Super Summer II		1988	2	4
	set of six: sand castle pail with shovel, sand pail with rake, fish sand mold, inflatable sailboat, beach ball, watering can			
Tale Spin		1990	2	4
	set of U3 toys: Baloo's seaplane, Wildcat's jet			

! Remember, prices given are for individual pieces only, not complete sets.

Teenie Beanie Babies, McDonald's, 1999.

The Busy World of Richard Scarry, McDonald's, 1995.

TOY NAME	DESCRIBE	YEAR	EX	MINT
Tale Spin		1990	2	4
	set of four characters in airplanes: Wildcat's Flying Machine, Baloo's Seaplane, Molly's Biplane, Kit's Racing Plane			
Tamagotchi Key Chains		1998	2	4
	set of nine: yellow, purple, green, red, blue with yellow figure inside, white with red figure inside, red/orange flip action, blue flashlight, purple #9 (only available at McDonald's in Wal-Mart stores)			
Teenie Beanie Babies		1997	5	10
	set of ten plush toys: Patti the Platypus, Pinky the Flamingo, Chops the Lamb, Chocolate the Moose, Goldie the Goldfish, Speed the Turtle, Seamore the Seal, Snort the Bull, Quack the Duck, Lizz the Lizard			
Teenie Beanie Babies		1998	2	4
	set of twelve plush toys: Doby the Doberman, Bongo the Monkey, Twigs the Giraffe, Inch the Worm, Pinchers the Lobster, Happy the Hippo, Mel the Koala, Scoop the Pelican, Bones the Dog, Zip the Cat, Waddle the Penguin, Peanut the Elephant			
Teenie Beanie Babies		1999	2	4
	set of twelve: Freckles the Leopard, Smoochy the Frog, Rocket the Blue Jay, Strut the Rooster, Claude the Crab, 'Nook the Husky, Antsy the Anteater, Spunky the Cocker Spaniel, Iggy the Iguana, Nuts the Squirrel, Stretchy the Ostrich, Chip the Cat			
Teenie Beanie Babies International Bears		1999	2	4
	set of four: Britania, Glory, Erin, Maple; over-the-counter promotion available for $1.99 with food purchase			
The Busy World of Richard Scarry		1995	1	2
	set of four: Lowly Worm and Post Office, Huckle Cat and School, Mr. Fumble and Fire Station, Bananas Gorilla and Grocery Store			
The Busy World of Richard Scarry		1995	1	2
	one U3 toy: Lowly Worm, rubber			
The Legend of Mulan		1998	1	2
	set of ten figures: Mulan, Khan, Mushu, Shanyu, Shang, Chein Po, Ying, Yao, Little Brother, Cri-Kee			

! Remember, prices given are for individual pieces only, not complete sets.

Tiny Toon Adventures Wacky Rollers, McDonald's, 1992. Photo courtesy Museum of Science and Industry, Chicago.

Tiny Toon Adventures Flip Cars Display, McDonald's, 1991.

TOY NAME	DESCRIBE	YEAR	EX	MINT

The Lion King II Simba's Pride
        set of eight: Kovu, Zazu, Timon, Simba,
    Kiara, Zira, Rafiki, Pumbaa
		1998	1	2

Tic Toc Mac Game yellow base, Grimace is X, Ronald is O		1981	2	5

Tonka/Cabbage Patch Kids, McDonald's, 1992.

Totally Toy Holiday, McDonald's, 1993.

! Remember, prices given are for individual pieces only, not complete sets.

Turbo Macs Insert, Birdie, the Early Bird, McDonald's.

Turbo Macs Insert, Grimace, McDonald's.

Turbo Macs Insert, Hamburglar, McDonald's.

Turbo Macs Insert, Ronald McDonald, McDonald's.

! Remember, prices given are for individual pieces only, not complete sets.

TOY NAME	DESCRIBE	YEAR	EX	MINT
Tinosaurs	set of eight figures: Link the Elf, Baby Jad, Merry Bones, Dinah, Time Traveller Fern, Tiny, Grumpy Spell, Kave Kolt Kobby; regionally distributed in St. Louis, Missouri	1986	5	10
Tiny Toon Adventures Flip Cars	set of four cars, each with two characters: Montana Max/Gobo Dodo, Babs/Plucky Duck, Hampton/Devil, Elmyra/Buster Bunny	1991	1	2
Tiny Toon Adventures Flip Cars	set of two U3 toys: Gogo Dodo in bathtub, Plucky Duck in red boat	1991	3	5
Tiny Toon Adventures Wacky Rollers	set of eight: Buster Bunny, Babs Bunny, Elmyra, Dizzy Devil, Gogo Dodo, Montana Max, Plucky Duck, Sweetie	1992	1	3
Tiny Toon Adventures Wacky Rollers	one U3 toy: Sweetie	1992	2	4
Tom & Jerry Band	set of four characters with musical instruments: Tom at keyboard, Jerry on drums, Spike on bass, Droopy at the mike	1990	4	8
Tom & Jerry Band	one U3 toy: Droopy	1990	5	8
Tonka/Cabbage Patch Kids	one U3 toy: Dump Truck	1992	1	2
Tonka/Cabbage Patch Kids	set of four: Crane, Loader, Grader, Bulldozer; joint promotion with Cabbage Patch Kids	1992	1	3
Tonka/Cabbage Patch Kids	set of five: Fire Truck, Loader, Cement Mixer, Dump Truck, Backhoe; joint promotion with Cabbage Patch Kids	1994	1	2
Tonka/Cabbage Patch Kids	one U3 toy: Dump Truck	1994	2	3
Toothbrush Happy Meal	set of three Ronald toothbrushes: red, yellow, blue	1985	20	40
Tops	set of three: red, blue and green	1978	3	7

TOY NAME	DESCRIBE	YEAR	EX	MINT
Totally Toy Holiday	set of three U3 toys: Keyforce Car, Magic Nursery Boy, Magic Nursery Boy	1993	2	3
Totally Toy Holiday	set of eleven: Lil' Miss Candistripes, Magic Nursery Boy, Magic Nursery Girl, Polly Pocket, Key Force Truck, Key Force Car, Mighty Max, Tattoo Machines, Attack Pack Vehicles, Caucasian Sally Secrets, African-American Sally Sercets	1993	2	3
Totally Toy Holiday	Holiday Barbie snow dome; recalled	1993	25	50

Walt Disney Home Video Masterpiece Collection: Toy Story case, The Three Caballeros case, McDonald's.

Walt Disney Home Video Masterpiece Collection: Toy Story's Woody figure, The Three Caballeros Donald Duck, McDonald's, 1997.

! Remember, prices given are for individual pieces only, not complete sets.

TOY NAME	DESCRIBE	YEAR	EX	MINT
Totally Toy Holiday	set of eight: Great Adventures Knight figurine with green dragon, Holiday Barbie, Hot Wheels Vehicle with ramp (came with red or green vehicle), "Once Upon a Dream" Princess figurine, Polly Pocket Playset, Mighty Max Playset, Cabbage Patch Playset, South Pole Explorer Vehicle	1995	1	2
Totally Toy Holiday	set of two U3 toys: Magic Nursery Boy, Magic Nursery Girl, Key Force Car	1995	3	5
Transformers Beast Wars/Littlest Pet Shop	set of four Transformer Beast Wars: Manta Ray, Beetle, Panther, Rhino; joint promotion with Littlest Pet Shop	1996	1	2
Transformers Beast Wars/Littlest Pet Shop	one U3 toy: Lion's Head Transformer	1996	1	2
Transformers/My Little Pony	set of twenty-six: Brawn—green/blue, blue/yellow, red/green, red/blue, red/yellow, green/yellow; Cliffjumper—red/black, burgundy/black, yellow/black, black/green, violet/blue, teal/black, black/blue; Bumblebee—black/red, burgundy/black, teal/black, violet/blue, black/green, yellow/black; Gears—green/yellow, green/blue, red/yellow, red/green, blue/yellow, red/blue; joint promotion with My Little Pony; regionally distributed in St. Louis, Missouri area	1985	50	140
Transformers/My Little Pony	set of three: Scorponok, Dinobot, Blackarachnia; split promotion with My Little Pony	1998	1	2
Turbo Macs	set of four: Birdie in pink car, Hamburglar in yellow car, Grimace in white car, Ronald in red car; test market Happy Meal	1988	5	10
Turbo Macs	one U3 toy: Ronald in red car with yellow wheels	1988	5	10
Turbo Macs	set of four: Ronald in red car, Grimace in white car, Birdie in pink car, Hamburglar in yellow car	1990	2	4

TOY NAME	DESCRIBE	YEAR	EX	MINT
Turbo Macs		1990	3	5
	one U3 toy: Ronald in red car with yellow wheels			
Under Sea		1980	2	3
	set of six cartons with undersea art: Alligator, Dolphin, Hammerhead Shark, Sea Turtle, Seal, Walrus			
VR Troopers		1996	1	2
	set of four: Visor, Wrist Spinner, Virtualizer, Kaleidoscope			
VR Troopers		1996	1	2
	one U3 toy: Sphere			
Walt Disney Home Video Masterpiece Collection		1996	1	2
	set of eight: Cinderella, Robin Hood, Pocahontas, Return to Jafar, Snow White, Sword and the Stone, Alice in Wonderland, Aristocats			
Walt Disney Home Video Masterpiece Collection		1996	2	4
	one U3 toy: Dumbo water squirter			

Front of World of Hot Wheels Bag, Gas Hog, McDonald's, 1994.

! Remember, prices given are for individual pieces only, not complete sets.

TOY NAME	DESCRIBE	YEAR	EX	MINT
Walt Disney Home Video Masterpiece Collection set of eight video cases with figure: Bambi with Bambi figure, The Lion King with Simba figure, Pete's Dragon with Elliot figure, Oliver and Company with Dodger figure, Toy Story with Woody figure, Sleeping Beauty with Sleeping Beauty figure, The Three Caballeros with Donald Duck figure, Winnie the Pooh with Tigger figure		1997	2	3
Water Games set of four: Birdie sorts eggs, Grimace juggles shakes, Ronald catches fries, Hamburglar stacks burgers		1992	3	5
Water Games one U3 toy: Grimace with squirting camera		1992	15	20
What is It? set of six rubber animals: Skunk, Squirrel, Bear, Owl, Baboon, Snake		1979	1	3
Wild Friends set of four animals on mini-comic books: Crocodile, Gorilla, Elephant, Panda; regionally distributed in Indiana and Southern California		1992	3	5
Wild Friends one U3 toy: soft rubber Giant Panda		1992	5	10
Winnie the Pooh Sing a Song with Pooh Bear set of eight: Eeyore, Owl, Winnie the Pooh, Rabbit, Roo, Piglet, Gopher, Tigger		1999	5	10
Winter World set of five flat vinyl tree ornaments: Ronald, Hamburglar, Grimace, Mayor McCheese, Birdie		1983	5	10
World of Hot Wheels/Friends of Barbie one U3 toy: Fast Forward		1994	2	3
World of Hot Wheels/Friends of Barbie set of eight: Turbine 4-2, Flame Rider, 2-Cool, Bold Eagle, Black Cat, Gas Hog, X21J Cruiser, Street Shocker; joint promotion with Barbie		1994	2	3
Wrist Wallets set of four watch-type bands with coin-holding dial: Ronald, Captain Crook, Big Mac, Hamburglar		1977	5	10

TOY NAME	DESCRIBE	YEAR	EX	MINT
Yo Yogi	set of four: Yogi Bear on wave jumper, Cindy Bear on scooter, Huckleberry Hound in race car, Boo Boo Bear on skate board	1992	3	5
Yo-Yo	half red, half yellow	1979	2	5
Young Astronauts	set of four snap-together models: Apollo Command Module, Argo Land Shuttle, Space Shuttle, Cirrus Vtol	1986	5	20
Young Astronauts	set of four vehicles: Space Shuttle & Space Walker, Command Module, Lunar Rover, Satalite Dish & Space Walker	1992	2	4
Young Astronauts	one U3 toy: Ronald in lunar rover	1992	2	4
Zoo Face I	set of four masks: Alligator, Monkey, Tiger, Toucan; test market Happy Meal, distributed in Evansville, Indiana	1987	20	30
Zoo Face II	set of four rubber noses and makeup kits: Alligator, Monkey, Tiger, Toucan	1988	5	10

Boxes

TOY NAME	DESCRIBE	YEAR	EX	MINT
Burger Six Pack to Go	"Six-Pack"	1989	5	10
Burger Six Pack to Go	McDonald's 6 2 Go	1989	5	10
Burger Six Pack to Go	Route 66 McDonald's	1990	5	10
Day & Night Happy Meal	two boxes: Ronald McDonald in All-Star Sunday, Ronald McDonald in Who's Afraid of the Dark; these boxes were not used with a specific promotion; generic premiums were included with Happy Meals	1985	3	5
Good Friends	set of two: A Clean Sweep, Snapshot Shuffle	1987	3	5

! Remember, prices given are for individual pieces only, not complete sets.

TOY NAME	DESCRIBE	YEAR	EX	MINT
Healing through Happiness		1995	10	15
Mulan		1998	3	5
Pizza Happy Sack	sack was used for the test market of McDonald's pizza and pizza Happy Meals	1991	15	20

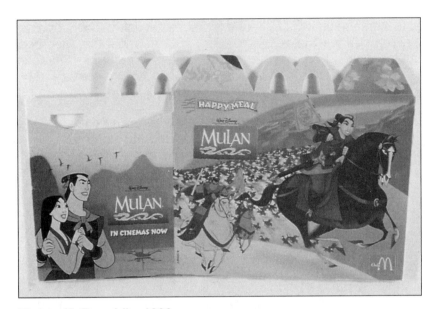

Mulan, McDonald's, 1998.

Burger Six Pack to Go, McDonald's, 1989.

Subway

Looking for a way to supplement his college tuition, Fred DeLuca borrowed $1,000 from Dr. Peter Buck, a family friend, to open Pete's Super Submarine, the predecessor of the Subway chain. Pete's Super Submarine was not an overnight success. It wasn't until they changed the name to Subway, opened a shop at a more visible location and increased their marketing effort that business finally took off. Today there are more than 14,000 Subway franchises around the world.

In order to increase their visibility and to help establish a family-oriented image, Subway developed their Kid's Pak meal in 1988. As most fast food chains have discovered, the most successful promotions are those featuring characters from a popular television program or movie. *The Simpsons*, *Coneheads*, Cracker Jacks and Jim Henson's *Bear in the Big Blue House* are a few of Subway's recent promotions.

Subway's first nationally advertised Kid's Pak promotion, Nickelodeon's *Blue's Clues*, was it's first network television-supported promotion. It was also Subway's most successful Kid's Pak premium to date, they are hoping to surpass its success with other licensed premiums like their recent Dexter's Laboratory promotion.

TOY NAME	DESCRIBE	YEAR	EX	MINT
Blue's Clues	set of four toys featuring characters from a special birthday episode of Nickelodeon's "Blue's Clues": Birthday Blue, Tickety Tock, Mailbox, Handy Dandy Notebook	1998	2	4
Cartoon Network	set of four toys featuring characters from The Flinstones and The Jetsons cartoons: Spinning Astro, Fred Flintmobile, Spaceage Wristband, Stoneage Wristband	1998	2	3
Cats Don't Dance	set of five toys based on characters from the animated film: Dancing Danny, Woolie Squirter, Sawyer, Pudge	1997	1	2
Clear Gear Cars	set of four clear plastic cars: Vantastik, Tractorsaurus Wrecks, Going Buggy, Tromper Truck	1997	1	2
Conehead Pencil Toppers	set of three: Beldar, Marlax, Prymaat	1993	2	3
Cracker Jack	set of four toys: Sailor Jack Compass, Sailor Jack Fan Whistle, Bingo Magnifying Glass, Cracker Jack Periscope	1999	2	3

! Remember, prices given are for individual pieces only, not complete sets.

Histeria!, Subway, 1999. Photo courtesy Subway.

Jim Henson's Bear in the Big Blue House, Subway, 1999.

TOY NAME	DESCRIBE	YEAR	EX	MINT
DC Super Heroes		1998	3	5
	set of four Super Hero backpack hangers: Superman, Batman, The Flash, Wonder Woman			
DinoStompers		1997	1	2
	set of four wind-up dinosaurs: Tyrannosaurus Rex, Parasaurolophus, Triceratops, Dimetroden			
Eek! Stravaganza		1997	2	4
	set of four toys: Eek! Fan Whistle, Annabelle Birthday Cake, Sharky the Dog Squirter, Eek! Squirter			
Histeria!		1999	1	3
	set of four toys featuring characters from the Kids' WB! television program: Twisty History Block, Miss Information Clip and Notepad, Histeria! Famous Moments Viewfinder, Histeria! Expedition Compass			

Kool-Aid, Subway, 1998. Photo courtesy Subway.

! Remember, prices given are for individual pieces only, not complete sets.

TOY NAME	DESCRIBE	YEAR	EX	MINT
Jim Henson's Bear in the Big Blue House	set of four: Big Blue House Viewfinder, Cha-Cha-Cha Bear, Pib & Pop Tub Fun, Tutter's Cheese Chase	1999	1	3
Kids' Pak Dough	set of four cans of molding dough with a tool: Yellow car set, red dinosaur set, blue funny face set, green dough cutter set	1998	2	3
Kool-Aid	set of three Kool-Aid toys: Activity cup, Kool-Aid Man mug, Connector straws	1998	1	3
Marvin the Martian	set of four back-to-school toys celebrating Marvin's 50th birthday: Ruler of the Universe, Spaceship Stamper Set, Galaxy Crayon Case, Clipboard and Notepad	1998	3	5
Nick Jr.	set of five toys: Flip Flop Blue, Detective Little Bear, My Friend Kipper, Dress-Up Maisy, Face's Play Sack	1999	1	2
Paulie	set of four toys based on this DreamWorks film: Whistling Paulie, Paulie Giggler, Wing-Flapping Paulie, RV Surprise	1998	1	2
Santa Claus	set of five: Sanat 3-D pzzle, ELFS action figre, Comet, snow globe twist puzzle, Santa Claus action figure	1994	2	3
Sea Splashers	set of four inflatable fish that also squirt water: Emperor Angelfish, Coral Trout, Clownfish, Stoplight Parrotfish	1997	1	2
Space Puzzles	set of four different outer space scenes featured on jigsaw puzzles	1997	1	2
Speed Bumpers	set of four pull-back cars: Blue Bumper, Purple Power, Blaze Racer, Lucky Lime	1997	1	2
Sports Illustrated for Kids	set of four sports toys: Soccer Sack, Super Baseball, Basketball flyer, mini football	1998	1	2
Stunt Racers	set of four die-cast cars with a stunt toy: Black car/ramp, red car/launcher, green car/road scene play mat, truck/crash wall	1998	1	2

TOY NAME	DESCRIBE	YEAR	EX	MINT
The King And I	set of four toys featuring characters from the animated film: Dancing King and Anna, Princess Ying Finger Puppet, Master Little, Tusker Finger Puppet	1999	1	2
The Simpsons	set of four figurines: Skateboarding Bart, Donut-Chasing Homer, Spinning Bartman, Musical Lisa	1997	3	5
Tom and Jerry	skateboard Tom, Beach Buggy Tom, Beach Buggy Jerry, Skateboard Jerry	1994	2	3

Nickelodeon's Nick Jr., Subway, 1999. Photo courtesy Subway.

! Remember, prices given are for individual pieces only, not complete sets.

Wendy's

Everyone has seen Dave Thomas, spokesman and founder of Wendy's, on television. With his TV spots, the Dave Thomas Foundation for Adoption and his involvement with local and national charitable organizations, Thomas is one of the most visible fast food entrepreneurs today. Even though Thomas was told the world didn't need another hamburger restaurant, he opened the first Wendy's in Columbus, Ohio, in 1969. Wendy's number two opened in 1970 where customers were able to pick up their food from a drive-up window with a separate grill. Ten years later in 1980, there were 2,000 Wendy's worldwide.

Little by little, Wendy's infiltrated the national psyche, and the über-successful "Where's the Beef" campaign in 1984 not only influenced a presidential candidate, it thrust the chain in to the forefront of national fast food spotlight, and by 1985, they had surpassed 3,000 restaurants.

It didn't take Wendy's long to jump on the fast food-toy bandwagon. In June 1983 they issued their first Kids' Meal which featured a spinning top, a glow-in-the-dark ball, an ABC/123 stencil and an invisible ink pen. The colorful packaging is some of the best in the industry, and the quality of their toys in the mid-eighties was superb, but went down hill in the early nineties. Their toys were resurrected in the eyes of collectors in 1996 when they offered set of six Felix the Cat toys. Not only did the toys feature a classic cartoon character, the quality of the set and packaging set them apart from anything Wendy's have done this decade.

TOY NAME	DESCRIBE	YEAR	EX	MINT
3-D Classic Comics	set of five comic books with 3-D glasses: Treasure Island with pink glasses, Call of the Wild with purple glasses, Robin Hood with silver glasses, King Arthur with green glasses, Swiss Family Robinson with blue glasses	1994	1	3
3-D color Classics	set of five: Gulliver's Travels, Peter pan, 20,000 Leagues Under the Sea, Peter Pan, The Time Machine, The Elephant's Child	1995	2	4
Alf Tales	set of six: Sleeping Alf, Alf Hood, Little Red Riding Alf, Alf of Arabia, Three Little Pigs, Sir Gordon of Melmac	1990	2	4
Alien Mix-Ups	set of six: Crimsonoid, Bluezoid, Limetoid, Spotasoid, Yellowboid, Purpapoid	1990	1	2
All Dogs Go To Heaven	set of six: Anne Marie, Carface, Charlie, Flo, Itchy, King Gator	1989	2	4

TOY NAME	DESCRIBE	YEAR	EX	MINT
American Youth Soccer Organization		1997	1	3
	set fo five: water bottle, kicker ball, footbag, inflatable soccer ball, trading cards			
Animalinks		1995	1	3
	set of five: octopus, monkey, giraffe, alligator, dog			
Ball Players		1995	1	3
	set of four: baseball, basketball, fottball, tennis			
Beach Planet		1998	1	3
	set of five: squeeze squirter, push squirter, inflatable drink holder, water bottle, beach ball			

Alf Tales, Wendy's, 1990.

Alf Tales Insert, Aladdin and his Magic Lamp, Wendy's, 1990.

❗ Remember, prices given are for individual pieces only, not complete sets.

Alf Tales Insert, Knights of the Round Table, Wendy's, 1990.

Alf Tales Insert, Robin Hood, Wendy's, 1990.

Alf Tales Insert, Sleeping Beauty, Wendy's, 1990.

TOY NAME	DESCRIBE	YEAR	EX	MINT
Bike Trax		1995	1	3
	set of five bicycle accessories: reflectors (2), water bottle, helmet stickers, bicycle pack, bicycle sign			
Book of Virtues		1998	1	3
	set of five: Plato coin purse, Socrates maze bookmark, jigsaw puzzle, Aristotle, color surprise poster			
Bruno the Kid		1997	1	3
	set of six: turbo craft, wrist pack, balancing plane, binocular car, sunscreen squirter, pencil decoder			
Carmen Sandiego		1994	2	4
	set of five: cup with secret compartment, book and secret binoculars, passport and travel kit, magnifying glass and pen, ruler and periscope			
Cartoon Network Wacky Racing		1999	2	4
	set of five: Jetson's pull-back car, Alligator sticker car, Yogi Bear freeroller, Dexter Popper car, Tom & Jerry bump-and-go car			

All Dogs Go To Heaven Insert, Anne Marie, Wendy's, 1990.

All Dogs Go To Heaven Insert, Carface, Wendy's, 1990.

! Remember, prices given are for individual pieces only, not complete sets.

All Dogs Go To Heaven Insert,
Charlie, Wendy's, 1989.

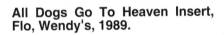

All Dogs Go To Heaven Insert,
Flo, Wendy's, 1989.

All Dogs Go To Heaven Insert,
Itchy, Wendy's, 1989.

TOY NAME	DESCRIBE	YEAR	EX	MINT
Cartoons		1996	1	3
	set of four: hot rod, bump 'n go, police car, split apart			
Club Cave		1997	1	3
	set of four: pick-up bones, sundail, dinosaur skeleton, dinosaur bank			
Cybersycles		1994	1	3
	set of five pull-back motorcycles: Eagle, Lightning, Gragon, Shark, Techno			
Cycle On		1997	1	3
	set of five bicycle accessories: bike bag, wrist reflector, license plate, stickers, water bottle			
Definitely Dinosaurs		1988	2	4
	set of four: blue Apatosaurus, gray T-Rex, yellow Anatosaurus, green Triceratops			
Definitely Dinosaurs		1989	2	4
	set of five: green Ankylosaurus, blue Parasaurolophus, green Ceratosaurus, yellow Stegosaurus, pink Apatosaurus			
Dexter's Laboratory		1997	1	3
	set of five: robotic arm, glow monster, color change straw, pen and stand, remote viewer			
Dino Games		1992	2	4
	set of five: Go Fish Dinos card game, Dino Maze, Dino Catch game, Dino Jam pinball game, Dino Obstacle Course game			

Definitely Dinosaurs, Wendy's, 1988-89.

! Remember, prices given are for individual pieces only, not complete sets.

Fast Food Racers, Wendy's, 1990.

All Dogs Go To Heaven
Insert, King Gator,
Wendy's, 1989.

Fast Food Racers
Insert, Wendy's, 1990.

Felix the Cat Insert, Ask Felix Toy,
Wendy's, 1996.

TOY NAME	DESCRIBE	YEAR	EX	MINT
Drinking Tubes	set of five straws: cup wrap, color change connector A, color connector B, rainbow, trumpet	1994	1	3
Eerie Indiana	set of five: wind-up hopping eyeball, crazy puzzle, door hanger, bone hand pen, evidence locker bank with secret compartment	1999	1	3
Endangered Animal Games	set of five: eagle catch game, mini puzzle, tiger pinball game, maze, crazy eight card game, mini puzzle	1993	2	4
Fast Food Racers	set of five: hamburger, fries, frosty, salad, kid's meal	1990	2	4
Felix the Cat	set of five: plush Felix, story board with drawing sheet and stylus, Ask Felix, zoetrope, milk caps and container	1996	2	4

Gear Up!, Wendy's, 1992.

Jetsons: The Movie Space Gliders Insert, George, Wendy's, 1990.

Speed Bumpers, Wendy's, 1992.

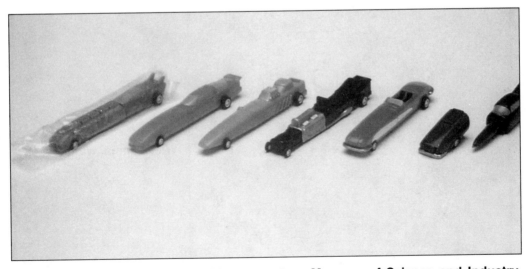

Speed Writers, Wendy's, 1991. Photo courtesy Museum of Science and Industry, Chicago.

TOY NAME	DESCRIBE	YEAR	EX	MINT
Felix the Cat	set fo five: Felix the Cat shoe laces, 3-D lenticular puzzle, Felix the Cat catch game, Felix the Cat adjustable trophy, plush Felix the Cat	1997	2	4
Fun Sips	set of five straws: spiral, connector A, glasses, connector B, buddy	1993	2	4
Furskins Plush Dolls	set of three: Boone in plaid shirt and red pants, Farrell in plaid shirt and blue jeans, Hattie in pink and white dress; all 7" tall	1988	4	8
Gear Up!	set of five bike accesories: saddle bag, handlebar streamers, reflector, license plate with stickers, water bottle	1992	2	3
Glo Friends	set of twelve: Book Bug, Bop Bug, Butterfly, Clutter Bug, Cricket, Doodle Bug, Globug, Granny Bug, Skunk Bug, Snail Bug, Snug Bug	1988	2	4
Glo Friends	set of twelve: Glo Snugbug, Glo Doodlebug, Glo Bug, Glo Grannybug, Glo Clutterbug, Glo Bashfulbug, Glo Butterfly, Glo Bopbug, Glo Cricket, Glo Skunkbug, Glo Bookbug	1989	1	2

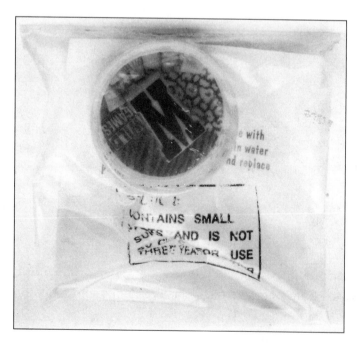

Wild Games, Wendy's, 1992.

! Remember, prices given are for individual pieces only, not complete sets.

TOY NAME	DESCRIBE	YEAR	EX	MINT
Glo-Ahead	set of five: slime glasses, stickers, pull-back racer, sucker figurine, flying dics and target	1993	2	4
Good Sports	set of five games: football, basketball, golf, bowling, hockey	1994	1	3
Good Stuff Gang	set of six: Cool Stuff, Cat, Hot Stuff, Overstuffed, Bear, Penguin	1985	2	4
Halloween Play-Doh Fingles	set of six: pumkin, ghost, cat, monster, bat, witch	1989	1	2
Halloween Play-Doh Fingles	set of six: pumkin, ghost, cat, monster, bat, witch	1990	1	3
Jetsons Figures	set of six figures in spaceships: George, Judy, Jane, Elroy, Astro, Spacely	1989	2	4
Jetsons: The Movie Space Gliders	set of six PVC figures on wheeled bases: Astro, Elroy, Judy, Fergie, Grunchee, George	1990	2	4
Kids 4 Parks	set of five: water bottle, magnifying glass, belt pouch, Nature's Notes journal, belt pouch	1993	2	4
Kratts' Creatures	set fo five: Jeep freeroller, wind-up ape, collector cars, field utensil, microscope	1997	1	3
Laser Knights	set of four: king, queen, warrior, dragon	1996	1	3
Laser Slates	set of eight: Seek & Find, Draw a Face, Tic-Tac-Toe, Outer Space, Animals, Costumes, Maize, Words	1989	1	2
Make Room	set of four: photo frame, poster calendar and stickers, door knob hanger, message pad	1995	1	3
Mega Wheel	set of four: rock star car, western wonder, 50s flash, wave wagon	1995	1	3

TOY NAME	DESCRIBE	YEAR	EX	MINT
Micro Machines Super Sky Carriers set of six kits: connect to form Super Sky Carrier		1990	2	4
Mighty Mouse set of six: Bat Bat, Cow, Mighty Mouse, Pearl Pureheart, Petey, Scrappy		1989	3	5
Muppets from Space set of five: Kermit doll keychain, Muppet bus viewer, Miss Piggy voice changer microphone, Gonzo Spaceship sparker, sticker activity book with mini movie paster		1999	2	4
NHL Kids set of five: wallet, pen holder, sticker book, pull-back racer, bank		1998	1	3
Pink and the Brain set of five: Red Reveal TV, note pad and pencil, brain lab, Popper spacecraft, mind control machine		1997	2	4
Play-Doh Fingles set of three finger puppet molding kits: green dough with black mold, blue dough with green mold, yellow dough with white mold		1989	3	6
Pocket Paks set of four mini neon bags: drawstring bag, wrist bag, backpack, barrel bag		1991	2	3
Potato Head Kids set of six: Captain Kid, Daisy, Nurse, Policeman, Slugger, Sparky		1987	4	8
Quest for Camelot set of five: castle viewer, Camelot passport, balancing Griffin, card game, pull-back Devon and Cornwall		1998	2	4
Robot Games set of four games: vocana, fall in hole, top and track, pinball		1996	1	3
Rocket Writers set of five pens: purple, yellow, green, pink, blue		1992	2	3
Sarus Sports Balls set of four: Footballasarus, Baseballasarus, Soccerasarus, Basketballasarus		1991	2	3

! Remember, prices given are for individual pieces only, not complete sets.

TOY NAME	DESCRIBE	YEAR	EX	MINT
Screamin'3-D color	set of five: nature, fun facts, adventures, wild rides, extreme sports	1996	1	3
Sharks	set of five: inflatable shark toy, inflatable shark viewer, squirt toy, wallet, water bottle	1996	1	3
Silly Sippers	set of five masks with straws: dog, pig, mustache, lips with tongue, funny lips	1991	2	3
Snoopy	set of five: Snoopy with light-up Woodstock, Snoopy's doghouse, Snoopy head viewer, Snoopy circus wheel, Snoopy magic writer	1998	2	4
Sonic Cucles	set of five: spider cycle, horse cycle, rocket cycle, dolphin cycle, flame cycle	1997	1	3
Speed Bumpers	set of five: Bump, Wow, Wildthing, Fun, Fly	1992	2	3
Speed Writers	set of six car-shaped pens: black, blue, fuchsia, green, orange, red	1991	2	4
Summer Fun	float pouch, sky saucer	1991	2	3
Sun Patrol	set of five: sailboat drink holder, cap, fish water bottle, pocket comb, beach ball	1994	1	3
Surprize	set of nine: pull-back dinosaur car, washale tatoos, froggie squirt toy, pull-back turtle, dinosaur michanical puppet, inflatable pterodactyl, critter rummy cards, clam telescope, Felix the Cat milk cap set	1995	2	4
Techno Tows	set of four: shovel tow, tow truck, 3-wheeler, boat carrier	1995	1	3
Teddy Ruxpin	set of five: Professor Newton Gimmick, Teddy, Wolly Whats-It, Fob, Grubby Worm	1987	3	10
Too Cool for School	set of five: hamburger notepad, pencil case with ruler, french fry address book, Frosty pencil sharpener with eraser, pickle pen	1992	2	4

TOY NAME	DESCRIBE	YEAR	EX	MINT
Tricky Tints		1992	2	3
	set of five: water bottle, set of three straws, iron-on, plastic visor, shoe laces			
Unbelievably Fun Objects (UFO)		1993	2	4
	set of five: glow-in-the-dark moon ball, glow-in-the-dark inflatable globe, comet ball, satalite sucker ball, Saturn ball			
Wacky Wind-Ups		1991	2	3
	set of five: Milk Shake, Biggie French Fry, Stuff Potato, Hamburger, Hamburger in box			
Way 2 Go		1996	1	3
	set of five: travel match game, water bottle, belt pouch, postcard booklet with pouch, travel log with stickers			
Where in the World is Carmen Sandiego		1996	2	4
	set of five: travel kit, travel viewer and spy mirror, flashlight and telescope, apple and decoder, gum pack and compass			
Where's the Beef Stickers		1984	1	3
	set of six			
Wild Games		1992	2	3
	set of five games: Target Shoot, Ski Pinball, Fry Box Aqua Catch, Basketball, Food Fun Aqua Catch			
Wishbone		1996	1	3
	set of five: book viewer, collector cards, pen, photobook with stickers, earth digger			
World Wildlife Foundation		1988	2	4
	set of four books: All About Koalas, All About Tigers, All About Snow Leopards, All About Pandas			
World Wildlife Foundation		1988	5	10
	set of four plush toys: Panda, Snow Leopard, Koala, Tiger			
Write and Sniff		1994	1	3
	set of five: cowboy with leather scent, beauty queen with rose scent, Hiker with pine scent, fireman with smoke scent, baseball player with grass scent			
Yogi Bear and Friends		1990	2	4
	set of six: Ranger Smith in kayak, Boo Boo on skateboard, Yogi on skates, Cindy on red scooter, Huckleberry in inner tube, Snagglepuss with surfboard			

! Remember, prices given are for individual pieces only, not complete sets.

TOY NAME	DESCRIBE	YEAR	EX	MINT

Boxes

TOY NAME	DESCRIBE	YEAR	EX	MINT
Alien Mix-Ups	connect-the-dot ship	1989	3	5
Definitely Dinosaurs!	with Playskool, with maze	1988	3	5
Definitely Dinosaurs!	with Playskool, with connect the dots	1988	3	5
Fun & Games with Wendy and the Good Stuff Gang		1988	3	5
Halloween Haunted House with Play-Doh		1989	5	10
The Adventures of the Four Nuggeteers	scrambled sauces and nugget note	1996	3	5
The Jetsons	Help George through Sky-Jam Maze	1989	5	10
Wendy and the Good Stuff Gang	Comic Strip	1985	5	10
Wendy and the Good Stuff Gang	Surprise Kids' Meal Box	1989	5	10
Wendy and the Good Stuff Gang watch their Garden Grow	Cool Stuff Made a Mistake	1988	5	10
Wendy and the Good Stuff Gang watch their Garden Grow	Wendy's Garden Riddles	1988	5	10
Yogi Bear and Friends	with maze	1990	5	10

Definitely   Dinosaurs!, Wendy's, 1988.

Fun & Games with Wendy and the Good Stuff Gang (front), Wendy's, 1988.

Fun & Games with Wendy and the Good Stuff Gang (back), Wendy's, 1988.

Halloween Haunted House with Play-Doh (front), Wendy's, 1989.

Halloween Haunted House with Play-Doh (back), Wendy's, 1989.

! Remember, prices given are for individual pieces only, not complete sets.

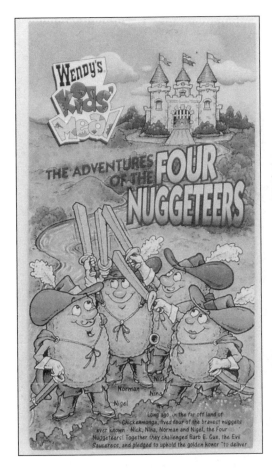

The Adventures of the Four Nuggeteers (front), Wendy's, 1996.

The Adventures of the Four Nuggeteers (back), Wendy's, 1996.

Wendy and the Good Stuff Gang (front), Wendy's, 1985.

Wendy and the Good Stuff Gang (back), Wendy's, 1985.

! Remember, prices given are for individual pieces only, not complete sets.

Wendy and the Good Stuff Gang watch their Garden Grow: Cool Stuff Made a Mistake (front), Wendy's, 1988.

Wendy and the Good Stuff Gang watch their Garden Grow: Cool Stuff Made a Mistake (back), Wendy's, 1988.

Wendy and the Good Stuff Gang watch their Garden Grow: Wendy's Garden Riddles (front), Wendy's, 1988.

Wendy and the Good Stuff Gang watch their Garden Grow: Wendy's Garden Riddles (back), Wendy's, 1988.

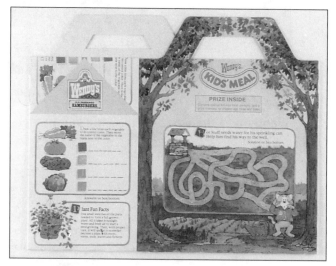

Wendy and the Good Stuff Gang, Wendy's, 1989.

White Castle

White Castle, the first "modern" fast food establishment in the country, opened in Wichita, Kansas in 1921. They sold little square burgers for 5-cents apiece and were destined to become a cult favorite. Known as gut bombs, grease balls and of course, Slyders, White Castle is probably the only fast food restaurant with a fan-club like website where at one point viewers are asked to "honor thy crave."

They were pioneers in the fast food business. In 1931 they introduced a crush-resistant container that kept their steamed burgers steaming and introduced the idea of take-out food to the burger fans everywhere. They were the first restaurant of its kind to issue coupons (five for the price of two). They lead the way for the McDonald's of the future.

By 1961, over one billion had been served. That number jumped to 2, 147, 176, 733 in 1968, more than any other fast food restaurant of the time.

It was in 1986 that White Castle introduced their Castle Meal. Over time they introduced their own characters, The Castle Meal Family. In 1990, they pulled off a spectacular set of toys: Fat Albert and the Cosby Kids. Well made and regionally distributed, this set was especially good for a regional chain.

White Castle has had a few well-made and popular promotions, but without the marketing clout of McDonald's they, along with most fast food restaurants, will never surpass the success of McDonald's.

TOY NAME	DESCRIBE	YEAR	EX	MINT
Ballerina's Tiara			3	6
Bendy Pens	set of five: Wilfred, Wobbles, Woofles, Woozy Wizard, Willis	1993	2	4
Camp White Castle			2	4
Camp White Castle Bowls	orange plastic		3	6
Castle Creatures			2	5
Castle Friends Bubble Makers	set of four	1992	3	5
Castle Meal Family	set of six: Princess Wilhelmina, Wendell, Sir Wincelot, Willis, Woozy Wizard, Woofles	1989	5	10
Castle Meal Family	set of five: Wilfred, King Wooly and Queen Winnevere, Wally, Wobbles and Woody, Friar Wack	1992	5	10

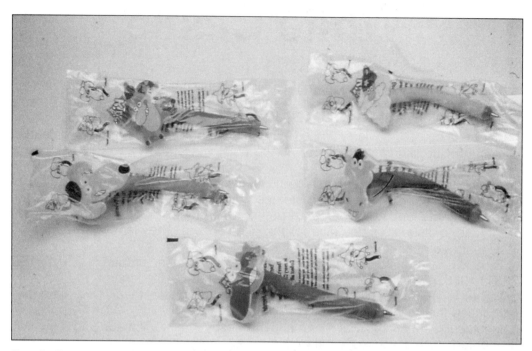

Bendy Pens, White Castle, 1993. Photo courtesy Museum of Science and Industry, Chicago.

Castle Meal Family Color Disks and Sticker, White Castle, 1989. Photo courtesy Museum of Science and Industry, Chicago.

! Remember, prices given are for individual pieces only, not complete sets.

TOY NAME	DESCRIBE	YEAR	EX	MINT
Castle Meal Family Color Disks and Sticker	set of four coloring page, crayon and puffy sticker: Friar Wack, Woofles, Princess Wilhelmina, Wobbles and Woody	1989	2	4
Castleburger Dudes Figures	set of four: Castleburger Dude, Castle Fry Dudette, Castle Drink Dude, Castle Cheeseburger Dude	1991	3	6
Castleburger Dudes Wind-up Toys	set of four: Castleburger Dude, Castle Fry Dudette, Castle Drink Dude, Castle Cheeseburger Dude	1991	3	6
Easter Pals	set of two: rabbit with carrot, rabbit with purse		3	5
Fat Albert and the Cosby Kids	set of four: Fat Albert, Dumb Donald, Russely, Weird Harold	1990	10	20
Food Squirters	set of three: Castle Fry Dudette, Castle Drink Dude, Castleburger Dude	1994	2	4
Glow in the Dark Monsters	set of three: Wolfman, Frankenstein, Dracula	1992	4	10
Godzilla Squirter			3	6

Castle Meal Family, White Castle, 1989. Photo courtesy Museum of Science and Industry, Chicago.

Castleburger Dudes Figures, White Castle, 1991. Photo courtesy Museum of Science and Industry, Chicago.

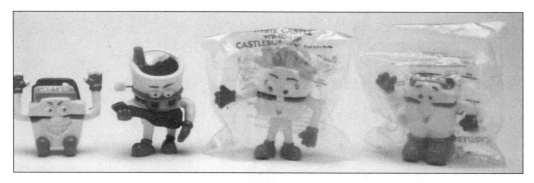

Castleburger Dudes Wind-up Toys, White Castle, 1991. Photo courtesy Museum of Science and Industry, Chicago.

Glow in the Dark Monsters, White Castle, 1992. Photo courtesy Museum of Science and Industry, Chicago.

! Remember, prices given are for individual pieces only, not complete sets.

TOY NAME	DESCRIBE	YEAR	EX	MINT
Halloween PEZ	set of three PEZ dispensers: Pumpkin, Witch, Skull	1990	2	4
Holiday Huggables	Candy Canine, Kitty Lights, Holly Hog		2	5
Nestle's Quik Rabbit	set of four: straw holder, spoon, cup, plush toy	1990	2	4
Puppy in My Pocket	set of twelve, two per package	1995	2	3
Silly Putty	set of three molds with Silly Putty: orange mold, yellow mold, green mold	1994	2	4
Stunt Grip Geckos	set of four figures: turquoise, pink, purple, blue	1992	2	4
Super Balls	set of four: Castleburger Dude, Castle Cheeseburger Dude, Castle Fry Dudette, Castle Drink Dude	1994	2	3
Swat Kats	set of three figures with launchers: Razor, T-Bone, Callie	1994	2	3
Tootsie Roll Express	set of four train cars: Engine, Gondola, Hopper, Caboose	1994	3	5

Tootsie Roll Express, White Castle, 1994. Photo courtesy Museum of Science and Industry, Chicago.

TOY NAME	DESCRIBE	YEAR	EX	MINT
Totally U Back To School			2	4
	set of two: pencil, pencil case			
Triastic Take-a-Parta		1994	2	3
	set of four: Megasaur, Spinasaur, Coolasaur, Sorasaur; also distributed by Carl's Jr.			
Water Balls		1993	2	3
	set of four: Castleburger Dude, Castle Cheeseburger Dude, Castle Fry Dudette, Castle Drink Dude			
Willis the Dragon			3	6
	Christmas giveaway			
Willis the Dragon Sunglasses			2	4

! Remember, prices given are for individual pieces only, not complete sets.

Miscellaneous

TOY NAME	DESCRIBE	YEAR	EX	MINT
A&W				
Boxes				
Playtown Meal blue		1988	4	8
Playtown Meal silver		1988	4	8

Playtown Meal, A&W, 1988.

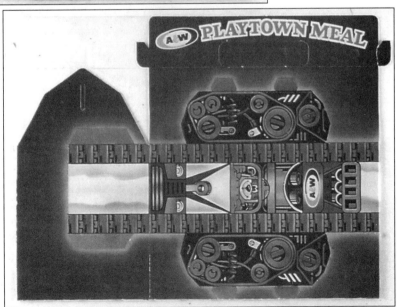

Playtown Meal, A&W, 1988.

TOY NAME	DESCRIBE	YEAR	EX	MINT

Big Boy

TOY NAME	DESCRIBE	YEAR	EX	MINT
Action Figures	complete set of four: skater, pitcher, surfer, race driver	1990	2	4
Big Boy Bank, Large	produced from 1966-1976, 18" tall, full color	1960s	125	300
Big Boy Bank, Medium	produced from 1966-1976, 9" tall, brown	1960s	50	165
Big Boy Bank, Small	produced from 1966-1976, 7" tall, painted red/white	1960s	40	100
Big Boy Board Game		1960s	50	120
Big Boy Kite	kite with image of Big Boy	1960s	10	25
Big Boy Nodder	papier-mâché	1960s	900	1500
Big Boy Playing Cards	produced in four designs	1960s	15	45
Big Boy Stuffed Dolls	set of three: Big Boy, girlfriend Dolly, both 12" tall, and dog Nuggets, 7" tall	1960s	40	80

Play Yard, Big Boy, 1992. Photo courtesy Museum of Science and Industry, Chicago.

! Remember, prices given are for individual pieces only, not complete sets.

TOY NAME	DESCRIBE	YEAR	EX	MINT

Big Boy (continued)

TOY NAME	DESCRIBE	YEAR	EX	MINT
Helicopters	set of plastic vehicles: Ambulance, Police, Fire Department	1991	1	3
Monster In My Pocket	various secret monster packs	1991	2	4
Play Yard	set of seven: strawberry, blueberry, grape, sandbox, slide, swing, teeter-totter	1992	5	10
Racers	set of three cars: yellow, orange, purple	1992	2	5
Sport Poses	set of four: surfing, baseball, racing, roller skating	1990	3	5

Racers, Big Boy, 1992. Photo courtesy Museum of Science and Industry, Chicago.

Sport Poses, Big Boy, 1990. Photo courtesy Museum of Science and Industry, Chicago.

TOY NAME	DESCRIBE	YEAR	EX	MINT

Carl's Jr.

50th Anniversary		1991	3	5
	set of four: Happy Star baseball, Happy Star plastic puzzle, Cruisin booklet, Groovy 60's jigsaw puzzle			
Addams Family Figure		1993	2	5
	set of five: Thing pencil topper, Lurch stamper, Cousin Itt Bubbles, The Addams Family Mansion and Stickers			
Camp California		1992	3	5
	set of four: Bear Squirter, Lil' Bro Disk, Mini Volleyball, Spinner; similar to set issued by Hardee's			
Camping with Woody Woodpecker		1991	5	10
	set of two: Andy Panda container, pen knife utensil kit			

Fender Bender 500, Carl's Jr., 1990. Photo courtesy Museum of Science and Industry, Chicago.

Muppet Parade of Stars, Carl's Jr., 1995. Photo courtesy Museum of Science and Industry, Chicago.

! Remember, prices given are for individual pieces only, not complete sets.

TOY NAME	DESCRIBE	YEAR	EX	MINT

Carl's Jr. (continued)

TOY NAME	DESCRIBE	YEAR	EX	MINT
Fender Bender 500	set of five: Yogi and Boo Boo, Huckleberry Hound and Snagglepuss, Magilla Gorilla and Wally Gator, Quick Draw McGraw and Baba Looey, Dick Dasterdly and Muttley; also issued by Hardee's	1990	3	5
Life Savers Roll 'Em	set of five: Pineapple, Cherry, Orange, Lemon, Lime	1990	4	8
Life Savers Roll 'Em	set of five: Pineapple, Cherry, Orange, Lemon, Lime	1995	1	2
Muppet Parade of Stars	set of four: Miss Piggy, Kermit Gonzo, Fozzy	1995	4	6
Starnaments	set of seven: Yellow star, Reindeer star, Snowman star, Elf Star, Chimney Sweep star, Toy Soldier star	1990	4	6
Starnaments	set of four: Anniversary star, Moose star, Holly star, Twinkle star	1991	4	6
Starnaments	set of five: Angel star, Mouse star, Toy Soldier star, Caroler star, Snow star	1992	4	6

Starnaments, Carl's Jr., 1990-92.

TOY NAME	DESCRIBE	YEAR	EX	MINT

Chick-Fil-A

Adventures in Odyssey Books set of seven: Mike Makes Right, The Treasure of La Monde, Isaac the Courageous, All's Well with Boswell, A Matter of Obedience, Last Great Adventure of Summer		1991	2	4
Adventures in Odyssey Cassette Tapes set of six: The Ill-Gotten Deed, This is Chad Pearson?, Wishful Thinking, A Test for Robin, Suspicious Minds, Father's Day		1993	3	6
On the Go set of six foam vehicles: car, airplane, train, truck, boat, helicopter		1993	1	2
Wonderful World of Kids		1995	2	5

Dairy Queen

Circus Train		1994	4	5
Dennis the Menace set of four: Dennis in fire truck, Margaret in astronaut suit, Ruff in dinosaur costume, Joey in race car		1993	4	6

Rock-A-Doodles, Dairy Queen, 1992. Photo courtesy Museum of Science and Industry, Chicago.

! Remember, prices given are for individual pieces only, not complete sets.

TOY NAME	DESCRIBE	YEAR	EX	MINT

Dairy Queen (continued)

TOY NAME	DESCRIBE	YEAR	EX	MINT
Dennis the Menace	set of four: Dennis, Margaret, Joey, Ruff; each cup featured images of individual character and a 3-D molded plastic cup lid	1993	4	6
Funbunch Flyer	each featured a different animal with the Dairy Queen logo		3	5
Holiday Bendies	set of four: Santa with open eyes, Santa with closed eyes, Reindeer with bell, Reindeer with scarf	1993	3	5
Rock-A-Doodles	set of six: Chanticleer, Patou, Edmund, Peepers, Peepers, The Grand Duke of Owl	1992	6	10
Rockin' Toppers	set of four pencil toppers: blue, yellow, green, red; rubber toppers with clingy surface allowing them to walk down walls	1993	1	2
Supersaurus Puzzles	set of three	1993	2	3
Tom and Jerry figures	set of six: Tom Squirter, Jerry Squirter, Tom Summer Cruiser, Jerry Summer Cruiser, Tom Stamper, Jerry Stamper	1993	4	6

Tom and Jerry figures, Dairy Queen, 1993. Photo courtesy Museum of Science and Industry, Chicago.

TOY NAME	DESCRIBE	YEAR	EX	MINT

Dairy Queen (continued)

Boxes

Funbunch Munch submarines and scubadivers		1	2
Funbunch Munch parachutes and airplanes		1	2

Funbunch Munch: parachutes and airplanes (front), Dairy Queen.

Funbunch Munch: parachutes and airplanes (back), Dairy Queen.

Funbunch Munch: submarines and scubadivers (front), Dairy Queen.

Funbunch Munch: submarines and scubadivers (back), Dairy Queen.

! Remember, prices given are for individual pieces only, not complete sets.

TOY NAME	DESCRIBE	YEAR	EX	MINT

Denny's

Dino-Makers		1991	1	2
	set of six: including blue dino, purple elephant, orange bird			
Flintstones Dino Racers		1991	3	6
	set of six: Fred, Bamm-Bamm, Dino, Pebbles, Barney, Wilma			
Flintstones Fun Squirters		1991	2	4
	set of six: Fred with telephone, Wilma with camera, Dino with flowers, Bam Bam with soda, Barney, Pebbles			
Flintstones Glacier Gliders		1990	2	4
	set of six: Bamm-Bamm, Barney, Fred, Dino, Hoppy, Pebbles			
Flintstones Mini Plush		1989	2	4
	set of four, in packages of two: Fred/Wilma, Betty/Barney, Dino/Hoppy, Pebbles/Bamm-Bamm			

Flintstones Dino Racers, Denny's, 1991. Photo courtesy Museum of Science and Industry, Chicago.

Flintstones Glacier Gliders, Denny's, 1990. Photo courtesy Museum of Science and Industry, Chicago.

TOY NAME	DESCRIBE	YEAR	EX	MINT

Denny's (continued)

Flintstones Rock 'n Rollers
        set of six: Fred with guitar, Barney with
        sax, Bam Bam, Dino with piano, Elephant,
        Pebbles
		1990	3	6

Flintstones Stone-Age Cruisers
        set of six: Fred in green car, Wilma in red
        car, Dino in blue car, Pebbles in in purple
        bird, Bam Bam in orange car, Barney in
        yellow car with sidecar
		1991	2	4

Flintstones Vehicles
        set of six: Fred, Wilma, Pebbles, Dino,
        Barney, Bamm-Bamm
		1990	2	4

Jetsons Crayon Fun Game
        set of six booklets with crayon game:
        George in Leisurly George, Jane in Jane
        Gets Decorated, Judy in Dream Date, Elroy
        What a Sport, Astro in Every Dog has his
        Daydream, Rosie in I Need Some Space
			2	4

Flintstones Rock 'n Rollers, Denny's, 1990. Photo courtesy Museum of Science and Industry, Chicago.

Jetsons Go Back to School, Denny's, 1992. Photo courtesy Museum of Science and Industry, Chicago.

! Remember, prices given are for individual pieces only, not complete sets.

TOY NAME	DESCRIBE	YEAR	EX	MINT

Denny's (continued)

Jetsons Game Packs		1992	2	4
	set of six: George, Elroy, Judy, Astro, Rosie, Jane			
Jetsons Go Back to School		1992	2	4
	set of six school tools: mini dictionary, folder, message board, pencil and topper, pencil box, triangle and curve			
Jetsons Puzzle Ornaments		1992	2	4
	set of six: Saturn with George, Earth with Jane, Jupiter with Judy, Mars with Elroy, Moon with Astro, Neptune with Rosie			
Jetsons Space Balls (Planets)		1992	2	4
	set of six: Jupiter, Neptune, Earth, Saturn, Mars, glow-in-the-dark Moon			
Jetsons Space Cards		1992	2	4
	set of five: Spacecraft, Phenomenon, Astronomers, Constellations, Planets			
Jetsons Space Travel Coloring Books		1992	2	4
	set of six books: each with four crayons			

Domino's Pizza

Noids		1987	2	4
	set of seven figures: Boxer, Clown, He Man, Holding Bomb, Holding Jack Hammer, Hunchback, Magician			
Quarterback Challenge Cards		1991	1	2
	pack of four cards			

International House of Pancakes

Pancake Kid dolls		1992	7	10
	set of three cloth dolls: Bonnie Blueberry, Susie Strawberry, Chocolate Chip Charlie			

Pancake Kids Cruisers, International House of Pancakes, 1993. Photo courtesy Museum of Science and Industry, Chicago.

TOY NAME	DESCRIBE	YEAR	EX	MINT

International House of Pancakes (continued)

Pancake Kids		1991	4	6
	set of ten: Cynthis Cinnamon Apple, Susie Strawberry, Bonnie Blueberry, Harvey Harvest, Betty Buttermilk, Frenchy, Rosana Banana Nut, Peter Potato, Von der Gus			
Pancake Kids Cruisers		1993	4	6
	set of eight: Von der Gus, Bonnie Blueberry, Susie Strawberry, Harvey Harvest, Chocolate Chip Charlie, Frenchy, Cynthia Cinnamon Apple, Betty Buttermilk			

Jack in the Box

Bendables		1980s	10	15
	set of five: Jack the Clown, Onion Ring Thing, Hamburger Meister, Secret Soft Agent, Small Fry			

Pancake Kids, International House of Pancakes, 1991. Photo courtesy Museum of Science and Industry, Chicago.

Bendables, Jack in the Box, 1991. Photo courtesy Museum of Science and Industry, Chicago.

! Remember, prices given are for individual pieces only, not complete sets.

TOY NAME	DESCRIBE	YEAR	EX	MINT

Jack in the Box (continued)

TOY NAME	DESCRIBE	YEAR	EX	MINT
Bendables		1991	2	3
	set of five: Jumbo Jack, red; Ollie O Ring, purple; Edgar E Eggroll, light blue; Sly Fry, red; Betty Burger, pink			
Bendables		1992	2	3
Jack Pack Finger Puppets		1993	2	3

Boxes

TOY NAME	DESCRIBE	YEAR	EX	MINT
Zany Space Buddies		1990	2	3

Zany Space Buddies (front), Jack in the Box, 1990.

Zany Space Buddies (back), Jack in the Box, 1990.

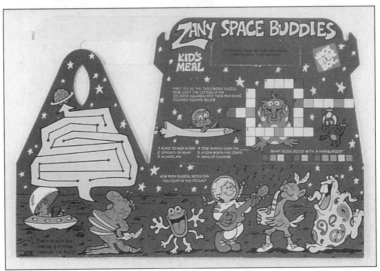

TOY NAME	DESCRIBE	YEAR	EX	MINT

Lee's Fried Chicken

Cartoon Viewers		1980s	20	50
	set of six: Mighty Mouse, Woody Woodpecker, Popeye, Superman, Bugs Bunny, Porky Pig			

Pizza Hut

Air Garfield		1993	2	4
	figure of Garfield attached to either a parachute or suspended in a spaceball			
Air Garfield Cups		1993	1	4
	set of two: each cup featured Garfield and Odie			
Beauty & the Beast Puppets		1992	4	8
	set of four: Belle, Beast, Chip, Cogsworth			
Color Your World		1993	4	6
	set includes erasable calendar board with four Crayons, poster with four Crayons; each meal came with plastic cup			
Dinosaurs!		1993	4	8
	set of four 16 oz. cups with 3-D lids and sticker books: Brachiosaurus, Tyrannosaurus, Stegosaurus, Brachiosaurus			
Eureeka's Castle Puppets		1991	3	6
	set of three: Batly, Eureeka, Magellan			

Land Before Time Puppets, Pizza Hut, 1988.

! Remember, prices given are for individual pieces only, not complete sets.

TOY NAME	DESCRIBE	YEAR	EX	MINT

Pizza Hut (continued)

TOY NAME	DESCRIBE	YEAR	EX	MINT
Fievel Goes West cups	set of three: Fievel with cowboy hat, Cat R. Waul with red top hat, Wylie Burp with tan hat	1991	4	6
Land Before Time Puppets	set of six: Spike, Sharptooth, Pteri, Little Foot, Cera, Ducky	1988	4	8
Marsupilami Houba Douba	set of three: yo-yo, jump rope, glow ball	1994	4	6
Star Wars Episode I, The Phantom Menace: Cup Toppers	set of four: Jar Jar, Mace Windu, Nute Gunray, Yoda	1999	2	3
Star Wars Episode I, The Phantom Menace: Planet Corscant	set of eight: Jar Jar Binks Squishy, Lott Dodd Walking Throne, Yoda's Jedi Destiny, Queen Amidala's Royal Starship, R2-D2, Planet Coruscant, Sith Holoprojector, Darth Maul's Sith Infiltrator	1999	3	5
Universal Monster Cups	set of three: holographic cards with 3-D cups		10	20
Young Indiana Jones Chronicles	set of three toys plus cups: magnifying glass, compass, telescope	1993	4	6

Beauty & the Beast Puppets, Pizza Hut, 1992. Photo courtesy Museum of Science and Industry, Chicago.

TOY NAME	DESCRIBE	YEAR	EX	MINT

Roy Rogers

TOY NAME	DESCRIBE	YEAR	EX	MINT
Critters	set of eight: blue eyes, yellow; blue eyes, orange; blue eyes, purple; blue eyes, red; yellow eyes, orange; yellow eyes, yellow; pink eyes, orange; pink eyes, purple	1990	1	2
Cup Critters	Elephant, Alligator, Frog, Bear, Pig, Beaver, Lion, Duck, Turtle	1994	2	5
Gator Tales	set of four: AV Gator, Investi-Gator, Flora Gator, Skater Gator	1989	4	6
Hide 'n Keep Dinos	set of three: Brontosaurus, Triceratops, Stegosaurus	1989	3	5
Ickky Stickky Bugs	set of sixteen: Centipede, Grasshopper, Worm, Spider	1989	2	3
Skateboard Kids Figures	set of four: Boy with red skateboard; Boy with orange skateboard, Boy with purple, Girl with blue skateboard	1989	3	5
Snorks	set of thirty version of the four characters: Allstar, Case, Dimmy, Tooter	1988	3	5
Star Searchers	set of four: Saucer, Robot, Vehicle, Shuttle	1990	2	3
Tatoo Heads		1995	2	5

Boxes

TOY NAME	DESCRIBE	YEAR	EX	MINT
Be a Sport	Holler Guy, Dunk Shot, Tackle, Huddle	1989	3	5
Be a Sport	Dribble, Circus Catch, Header, Catcher	1989	3	5
Be a Sport	Bicycle Kick, Pitcher, Jump Shot, Angle Block	1989	3	5
Be a Sport	Clipping, Thigh Trap, Switch Hitter, Hot Hand	1989	3	5
Fun Flyers Airport	Fun Flyers Matching Game	1987	3	5

! Remember, prices given are for individual pieces only, not complete sets.

TOY NAME	DESCRIBE	YEAR	EX	MINT

Roy Rogers (continued)

TOY NAME / DESCRIBE	YEAR	EX	MINT
Fun Flyers Airport Help the Fun Flyer Find His Suitcase	1987	3	5
Ickky Stickky Buggs blue spider/number of bug eyes	1987	3	5
Ickky Stickky Buggs green grasshoppers/worm maze	1987	3	5
Ickky Stickky Buggs orange and brown caterpillar/buggs code	1987	3	5
Ickky Stickky Buggs pink caterpillar/caterpillar connect the dots	1987	3	5
Star Searchers black hole maze/robot connect-the-dot		3	5

Be a Sport: Clipping, Thigh Trap, Switch Hitter, Hot Hand (front), Roy Rogers, 1989.

Be a Sport: Clipping, Thigh Trap, Switch Hitter, Hot Hand (back), Roy Rogers, 1989.

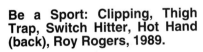

Be a Sport: Dribble, Circus Catch, Header, Catcher (front), Roy Rogers, 1989.

Be a Sport: Dribble, Circus Catch, Header, Catcher (back), Roy Rogers, 1989.

! Remember, prices given are for individual pieces only, not complete sets.

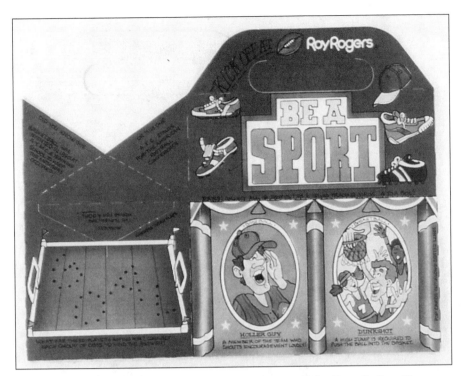

Be a Sport: Holler Guy, Dunk Shot, Tackle, Huddle (front), Roy Rogers, 1989.

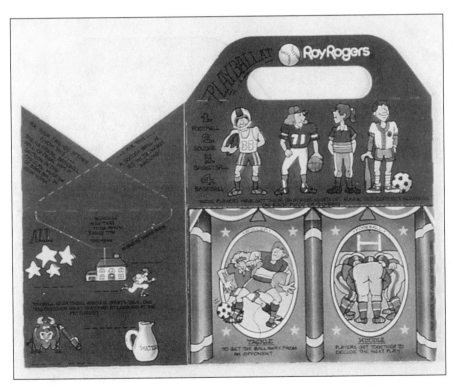

Be a Sport: Holler Guy, Dunk Shot, Tackle, Huddle (back), Roy Rogers, 1989.

Fun Flyers Airport: Fun Flyers Matching Game (front), Roy Rogers, 1987.

Fun Flyers Airport: Fun Flyers Matching Game (back), Roy Rogers, 1989.

! Remember, prices given are for individual pieces only, not complete sets.

Fun Flyers Airport: Help the Fun Flyer Find His Suitcase (front), Roy Rogers, 1987.

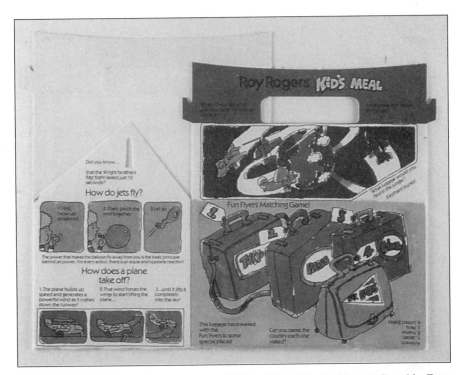

Fun Flyers Airport: Help the Fun Flyer Find His Suitcase (back), Roy Rogers, 1987.

Ickky Stickky Buggs: blue spider (front), Roy Rogers, 1987.

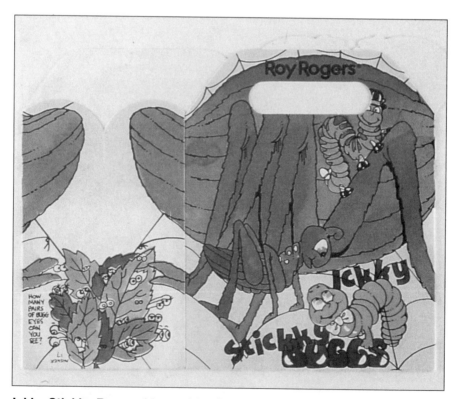

Ickky Stickky Buggs: blue spider (back), Roy Rogers, 1987.

! Remember, prices given are for individual pieces only, not complete sets.

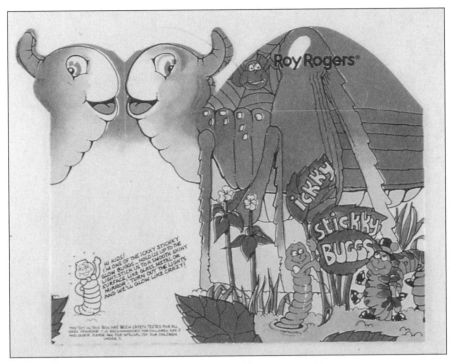

Ickky Stickky Buggs: green grasshoppers (front), Roy Rogers, 1987.

Ickky Stickky Buggs: green grasshoppers (back), Roy Rogers, 1987.

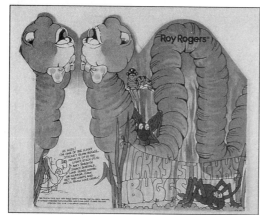

Ickky Stickky Buggs: pink caterpillar (front), Roy Rogers, 1987.

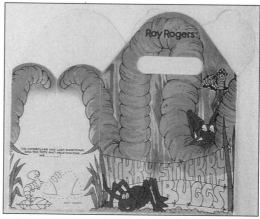

Ickky Stickky Buggs: pink caterpillar (back), Roy Rogers, 1987.

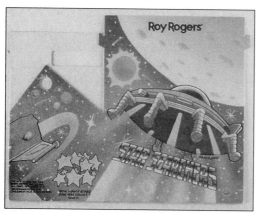

Star Searchers: black hole maze (front), Roy Rogers.

Star Searchers: black hole maze (back), Roy Rogers.

! Remember, prices given are for individual pieces only, not complete sets.

Sonic Drive-In

TOY NAME	DESCRIBE	YEAR	EX	MINT
Bag-A-Wag	set of four: man with bag of burgers in hamburger car, man with bag of burgers walking, man with bag of burgers rollerblading, man with hamburger	1990	3	6
Brown Bag Bowlers	set of four brown bag figures holding ball: yellow ball, red ball, blue ball, orange ball	1994	3	5
Brown Bag Buddies	set of four brown bag figures with sports equipment: sled, skiis, surfboard, intertube	1993	2	5
Brown Bag Juniors	set of four brown bag figures: Too Cool, Bookworm, Sure Shot, Marbles	1989	4	6
Bump and Go	series of 2" metal cars	1993	2	5
Custom Cruisers	set of four: Mercury, Chevy Convertible, Chevy Nomad, Cadillac Convertible	1993	3	5
Dino Makers		1994	2	5
		1989	5	8
Sonic Super Kids	set of four with comic book: Steve, Rick, Corky, Brin			
Sonic Turbo Racers	set of four: pink, yellow, orange, green	1993	2	5
Wacky Sackers	set of six: pink with bug-eyes, green with sunglasses, yelow, pink with three eyes, blue	1994	3	5

Brown Bag Bowlers, Sonic Drive-In, 1994. Photo courtesy Museum of Science and Industry, Chicago.

TOY NAME	DESCRIBE	YEAR	EX	MINT

Taco Bell

TOY NAME	DESCRIBE	YEAR	EX	MINT
Chihuahua Plush	set of four talking dogs: standing, says "Yo Quiero Taco Bell"; sitting with Free Tacos sign, says "Here Lizard, Lizard"; sitting wearing beret, says: "Viva Gorditas"; lying down wearing Santa hat, says: "Feliz Navidad Amigos"	1999	3	7
Happy Talk Sprites	set of two: Spark, yellow; Twink, white		2	4
Hugga Bunch Plush Dolls			2	4
Star Wars	set of seven: Death Star Spinner, Darth Vader/Yoda 3-D Cube, multi-scene cube, Bespin Cloud City, balancing Boba Fett, Millennium Falcon, R2-D2	1997	3	5
Star Wars Episode I, The Phantom Menace: Cup Toppers	set of four: Anakin, Darth Maul, Sebulba, Watto	1999	2	3

Star Wars, Taco Bell, 1997.

! Remember, prices given are for individual pieces only, not complete sets.

TOY NAME	DESCRIBE	YEAR	EX	MINT

Taco Bell (continued)

Star Wars Episode I, The Phantom Menace: Planet Tatooine		1999	3	5
	set of ten: Anakin's Podracer, Planet Tatooine, Walking Sebulba, Darth Maul's Sith Speeder, Hovering Watto, Joking Jar Jar Binks, Sebula's Podracer, Levitating Queen Amidala's Royal Starship, Anakin Skywalker Transforming Bank, Anakin Viewer, Sith Probe Droid Viewer			

Boxes

Kid's Fiesta Meal		1987	3	5
	Mercer Meyer New Little Critter's Bedtime Storybook			
Kid's Fiesta Meal		1987	3	5
	Dynomite Dinosaur			
Kid's Fiesta Meal		1993	3	5
	Dinosaur Days			

Kid's Fiesta Meal, Taco Bell, 1987.

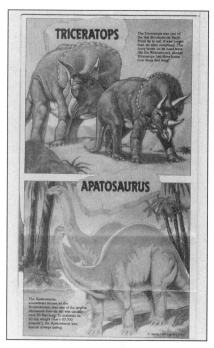

Kid's Fiesta Meal: Dinosaur Days (front), Taco Bell, 1993.

Kid's Fiesta Meal: Dinosaur Days (back), Taco Bell, 1993.

Kid's Fiesta Meal: Dynomite Dinosaur (front), Taco Bell, 1987.

Kid's Fiesta Meal: Dynomite Dinosaur (back), Taco Bell, 1987.

! Remember, prices given are for individual pieces only, not complete sets.

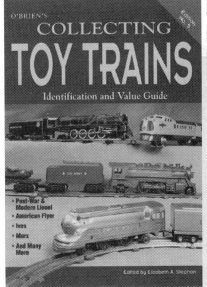

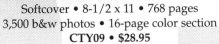
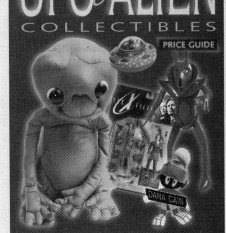

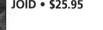
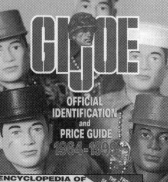